DATE DUE	BORROWER'S NAME	ROOM NO
FEB 2 00		
NO 1 2 '15		

92
JON

Flynn, Jean.   4035

Anson Jones : the
last president of
the Republic of
Texas

Anson Jones

The Last President of the Republic of Texas

by Jean Flynn

Illustrated by
Mark Mitchell

EAKIN PRESS ★ Austin, Texas

For my brothers, John and Jim,
and in memory of Bill.

Flynn, Jean
      Anson Jones : the last president of the Republic of Texas / by Jean
      Flynn.
         p.   cm.
      Includes bibliographical references (p.   ).
      Summary: Biography of doctor, farmer, and politician Anson
Jones, who served as the last president of the Republic of Texas and
was instrumental in bringing Texas into the union.
      ISBN 1-57168-106-X
      1. Jones, Anson, 1798-1858—Juvenile literature. 2. Presidents—
Texas—Biography—Juvenile literature. 3. Texas—History—Republic,
1836-1846—Juvenile literature. [1. Jones, Anson, 1798-1858.
2. Presidents —Texas.]   I. Title.
      F390.J76F58   1996
      976.4'04'092 — dc20
      [B]   96-24035
                                                                      CIP
                                                                       AC

Contents

A Note from the Author

I am greatly indebted to Herbert Gambrell, author of *Anson Jones: The Last President of Texas.* The book, first published in 1948 and revised with annotation and enlarged bibliography in 1968, is the most comprehensive study of Anson Jones available to researchers. Although I read many of the sources cited in Gambrell's bibliography, I could find no new insight into Dr. Jones' life.

All of the direct quotes in this manuscript come from Anson Jones' *Memoranda and Official Correspondence Relating to the Republic of Texas and Annexation, Including a Brief Autobiography of the Author.* I referred to *Memoranda* for cross-reference on sources listed in the bibliography. I also read the personal letters that are available in the Anson Jones Collection at the Center for American History at the University of Texas.

In summarizing his life and accomplishments, I hope I have done justice to Dr. Anson Jones, Architect of Annexation.

Chapter 1

The Young Student

"I studied with my book on the bench before me, while at work making harness . . . ."

Anson Jones disliked playing games as a child. He preferred the solitude of reading and studying. But fate determined the destiny of the shy and timid boy was to be interwoven with the destiny of a turbulent land called Texas.

Anson was the thirteenth child of fourteen children born to Solomon and Sarah Strong Jones. He was born on January 20, 1798, at Seekonkville, Great Barrington, Massachusetts. Ten of his brothers and sisters survived infancy: Sarah, Sophia, Mary, Nancy, Betsey, Clarissa, William, Ira, Anson, and Almira. Four children died at birth or soon after. Five-year-old Nancy fell from a bridge near the Joneses' house and drowned in the mill stream just after Anson's birth.

Solomon Jones was a tenant farmer and tanner. He had to move often to support his large family. The family moved ten times within Berkshire County during the first eighteen years of Anson's life. His first six or seven years were spent in a "pleasant little village in Berkshire County on the banks of the Housatonic." The town was originally settled by the Dutch in 1730, but by the end of the century most of its residents were farmers of English descent.

In 1805 Solomon moved his family to the country part of the township, an area known as "Root Street." He rented a small farm there.

While Anson's early years were bleak and drab, his life was much like that of others who grew up during the early 1800s. His parents, an honest and industrious couple, worked hard to scratch out a living from the soil of western Massachusetts.

Not all of the Jones family were poor. Anson's first American ancestor was William Jones. William served as deputy governor of New Haven and Connecticut for fifteen years ending in 1698 — one hundred years before Anson's birth. As an adult, Anson traced his family line back to Thomas Cromwell and John Hampden. The Cromwell coat of arms was eventually engraved on his table service.

Solomon Jones, Anson's father, was left an orphan at the age of seven. He became a young adult during the time of the American Revolution without any financial support or inheritance and was never able to buy much property. He was barely able to support his growing family. All of the children helped as they grew old enough.

When he was quite young, Anson attended a country school taught by his sister Sarah. The schoolhouse was almost a mile from where they lived. In the small country school he began the foundation for years of reading and study. Later he walked five miles every day to attend a more advanced school in Egremont Plains. He made the trip in summer and winter, regardless of the weather. When he was ten or eleven he finished his English studies under the guidance of the Episcopal rector, the Rev. Mr. Griswold, at Great Barrington.

Anson was fourteen when America's war with England began in 1812. He was eager to defend Boston against the British Redcoats. His father had served in the United States army during the Revolutionary War in 1775 and had fought in the defense of Bunker Hill. All of Solomon's brothers had served in the Revolutionary War. Two of them had been captured by the British and barely survived the horror of the "Jersey prison-ship." One of Anson's uncles had lost a leg during the war. When Anson volunteered to join the army, his father stopped him from going.

In 1812 Solomon moved his family to Lenox, the seat of Berkshire County. Anson was sent to Lenox Academy. One term at the academy ended his formal education. He later wrote: "My father being very poor, I was obliged to work and assist him in his business, and attend to my studies as I could find leisure and opportunity . . . . I studied with my book on the bench before me, while at work making harness, and obtained much of my education at 'night schools,' after working hard all day."

Even as a child Anson was not fond of playing and never learned the easy give-and-take of children at play. But he did like reading and studying. He was not in general good health and was considered the most delicate member of the large family. His brothers and sisters protected him from any hard, physical labor.

When his mother died, he realized how poor his father was. At the age of eighteen, he knew he had to choose a vocation.

Anson's brothers wanted him to learn a trade. After visiting the Pittsfield *Sun*, he decided he wanted to become a printer. The job did not require a great deal of physical strength and offered opportunities to read and study. His father and three older sisters wanted the youngest son in the family to become a physician. The choice of a career was not made by him but for him by his father and sisters.

"Notwithstanding I expressed my preference for this business [printing]," he wrote, "it was concluded that I should study medicine." Almost a year passed before he agreed to follow their wishes, which he said "entailed years of unhappiness." A shy and timid young man, he doubted his ability to become a physician. He had no knowledge of the world and no wealthy friends to help him. He was physically weak, and he lacked a well-rounded education to help him in his study of medicine.

Anson's father and sisters would not change their minds, even though his brothers continued to argue with them.

At the age of eighteen, Anson was committed to study medicine. Thirty years later, Anson said, "If it [the decision] were to make again I certainly should take a different course. Nor would I ever advise a youth, situated as I was, to make the choice I did, for, although some do succeed under such circumstances

4

. . . success I should say, by my experience, is too dearly purchased."

In 1817, full of self-doubt and worries about his future, Anson left his father's house. He went to stay with his sisters in Litchfield, Connecticut, and began his professional studies. He saw his father only twice more before Solomon Jones died in 1822.

There were few medical schools for training physicians in the early 1800s. The apprentice system was used for teaching. Anson became an apprentice to Dr. Daniel Sheldon of Litchfield. Dr. Sheldon, a practitioner, had been trained in the same manner. Anson assisted in setting broken bones, mixing drugs, sweeping floors, keeping records, tending the doctor's horses, and reading medical materials in his library. After a year with Dr. Sheldon, Anson had mounting debts and decided to give up his studies temporarily. He had not had a good year.

Anson became a teacher at nearby Goshen, but he continued to read as many medical books as he could borrow. At the end of his teaching year, he joined his brother William in Utica. William had opened a family grocery store with very little money and offered Anson his board for clerking in the store. He allowed Anson to study medicine under Dr. Amos G. Hull's supervision during Anson's spare time.

Mounting debts again drove Anson back to teaching. Besides that, William could no longer afford to have a clerk nor could he afford to house and feed Anson. After another year of teaching, Anson made arrangements to board on credit so he could study under Dr. Hull at Utica. He gave his undivided attention to study. Not only did he progress satisfactorily but he won a lifelong friend in his mentor, Dr. Hull. Dr. Hull, who supervised as many apprentices as he could, was widely respected and admired for his ability as a physician.

After two years of apprenticeship under Dr. Hull's guidance, Anson Jones was "examined and approved relating to his knowledge of physic and surgery." On September 5, 1820, he received the title of "Doctor." For the examination he paid the president of the Oneida Medical Society five dollars. Two dollars went to the treasury of the society, and each of the three examiners received one dollar.

The young doctor now had a license to practice for a fee. He felt secure in his future.

Chapter 2

The Poor Doctor

"I was arrested by one of my creditors and gave up my watch and the last dollar I had in the world but twenty . . . ."

Dr. Anson Jones went to Bainbridge, Connecticut, to hang his new shingle. Unable to afford an office by himself, he shared an office with lawyer William S. Stow. Stow, also new to the area, had many clients. He also had beautiful, expensive office furniture.

Jones bought a cheap, secondhand pine desk and made one office chair out of the parts of two broken ones. He sat day after day, hoping some of Stow's clients would need medical advice as well as legal advice. But Stow's clients continued to consult the old and experienced physician in town instead of twenty-two-year-old Dr. Jones. His debts grew daily, but he stuck it out for a year.

During the year in Bainbridge, Jones became acquainted with F. A. DeZeng, Esquire, as he called himself. DeZeng's house was the social center of the community. Jones and lawyer Stow were often invited to DeZeng's gatherings. While they were impressed with the older man's stories of the days when he was a baron of the Holy Roman Empire, Jones and Stow were more impressed with his lovely daughter. Both young men called to court the "belle of the county." When DeZeng chose Stow to be his son-in-law, Jones saw no reason to stay in Bainbridge. He had no prospects there, professional or personal.

He left everything behind when he moved to Norwich to open a drugstore. Dr. Hull, his mentor and friend, helped him get credit to stock the store. He hoped that he could gradually build up a medical practice along with his store. He was just beginning to feel secure personally and financially when he was sued by his former landlord.

J. E. Hinman, his landlord at Utica, felt Jones was prosperous enough to pay off his debts. He sued and got judgment to be paid for what was owed as well as all lawyer and court costs. The sheriff seized all of Jones' stock in the drugstore. Jones' New York creditors refused further credit. DeZeng, the old baron and friend, came to Jones' rescue. He bought the store's stock of drugs, and Jones finally settled his debts with Hinman.

Jones had other debt settlements against him that he would somehow have to pay. He returned again to medicine because no money was required to start a practice. His medical license was his only asset.

He chose Harpers Ferry in western Virginia to set up practice. Harpers Ferry was a small place with few physicians. There would be little competition, and his debtors would be unlikely to locate him there. Unfortunately for Jones, he had to pass through Philadelphia to go to Harpers Ferry from Norwich. He was arrested in Philadelphia by one of his creditors for outstanding debts.

Philadelphia, the "City of Brotherly Love," was no longer the capital of the United States in 1823. But it was the second largest city and the principal seaport of the nation. It also had a reputation for a growing medical center with a small group of physicians in practice.

Jones opened an office without delay in his living quarters. The tin sign above his door read "Anson Jones, Physician and Surgeon." No one came. Physicians beginning a new practice had to rely on referrals from friends and colleagues. He had never learned how to become a part of society. His shyness kept him from making a wide circle of friends. He was not outgoing in personality or striking in looks. People did not snub him; they just didn't notice him. He found no "brotherly love" in Philadelphia.

After a few months of not making expenses, Jones turned to teaching to support himself. He did not find teaching interesting and soon grew tired of it. Six months after he began, he received an offer to go to South America. Mr. Lowry, the American consul for Laguayra, made the offer. Jones quit his teaching job and took passage on the *Coulter* to Venezuela in the fall of 1824.

Anson Jones was so caught up in his own problems that he ignored two rumors that would later influence his life. One rumor concerned the training of physicians. Dr. George McClellan had planned a new medical school and was trying to get it approved by the legislature. The second rumor was that Southern farmers were moving into the Mexican province of Texas and land was available to those who wanted to apply for it.

Jones was focused on Venezuela, the center of South American independence. He made his home in Caracas, an independent republic. For two years he had a successful medical practice and was able to save "a few hundred dollars." He returned to Philadelphia on the *Coulter*, the same ship he had sailed on two years earlier. But the young man who returned was quite different from the one who had sailed. Jones not only had money, but for the first time in his life he felt successful and needed.

With his newfound self-confidence and a small savings, he rented an office and stocked it with drugs and medical instruments. Jones thought he was well-trained for his profession. What he found in Philadelphia in 1826 was an abundance of university-trained physicians. Jones' training ranked only a little higher than that of pharmacists and midwives.

When few patients came to him, he decided to finish his professional studies before his money ran out. Dr. McClellan had established Jefferson Medical College, a branch of the University of Pennsylvania. In March 1826, the medical college had conferred degrees on its first class of twenty physicians.

The college had a shaky beginning. Dr. McClellan rented a dilapidated building and called together six physicians he wanted on his faculty. He told the professors to donate $20 each to remodel the old building. The building, a short walk from Jones' new office, had been a cotton factory and then the

Tivoli Theater. The $120 that the professors spent on remodeling did little to improve the building.

Dr. McClellan's collegiate surgical clinic was the first in the United States. His students sat in opera chairs to observe. They went to the "green room" (a term used for the room where actors take breaks when they aren't on stage) to take their exams. Physicians who were not on the faculty predicted that the medical school would not last long.

Jones chose to enter Jefferson Medical College in the fall of 1826. No one recognized his ability to achieve distinction in his lifetime. He was just a timid licensed practitioner, nearing thirty, who sat in his office alone after school hours.

Ten years after Jones began his medical studies, he graduated from a medical college at a cost of less than $100. The college was still the target of jokes, but he had trained under "as competent instructors as any similar number of teachers in the schools of the country at that period": Doctors George McClellan, John Eberle, Jacky Green, William P. Barton, Nathaniel Chapman, and Benjamin Rush Rhees.

He finished his degree and turned his energies to attracting paying clients. He did not form a partnership nor make friends with other physicians, as was the custom of the times. He decided to meet new people by becoming a member of a Masonic Lodge.

Jones found he had a talent for understanding problems and finding a solution to them. He quickly moved up in the ranks of the fraternity. He also joined Odd Fellows and spent four or five evenings a week in Grand Lodge business. He served on practically every committee. While he learned how to sway men on a one-to-one basis, he did not learn how to persuade groups of men.

Although his popularity in the fraternities grew, his medical practice stood still. His fraternity brothers preferred a physician who devoted his whole life to healing. When the Odd Fellows began bickering among themselves, Jones resigned as Grand Master.

He took inventory of his life. Every year since he returned from Venezuela, his expenses were more than his income. He lost the self-confidence he had gained in Caracas. He decided to leave Philadelphia and the medical profession behind. Anson Jones looked south for a business venture.

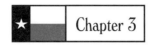 Chapter 3

Sailing South

". . . in October, 1832, [I] sailed from New York in the ship Alabama *for New Orleans."*

Anson Jones had lost his enthusiasm for medicine. When Thomas J. Spear, a merchant in Philadelphia, wanted to extend his business to New Orleans, he offered Jones a partnership. He asked Jones to become the senior partner of a mercantile house to be named Jones & Spear. Jones was to be the resident director in New Orleans.

On October 10, 1832, he sailed on the *Alabama* after supervising the loading of his merchandise. On the trip the *Alabama* lost five sails and one man and drifted for days. It took twenty-nine days to reach New Orleans.

During the time the *Alabama* was trying to reach its destination, a cholera epidemic reached New Orleans. When Jones chose the city, the population was more than 50,000. When he arrived there, it was less than 30,000. Yellow fever had driven away 16,000 people. Another 6,000 people had died of cholera within twelve days.

14

The day of Jones' arrival, he read in the *Louisiana Advertiser* that the city was "becoming, every day, more and more restored, the bustle and activity, to which we are accustomed, will shortly be resumed." The sun was shining for the first time in two weeks. People were optimistic that the epidemic was over because there had been only fifty-seven burials the day before.

It was in this city of chaos that Jones found himself stranded with no money and many debts. Credit for the Jones & Spear business had been granted in Anson Jones' name, as he was the senior partner. Thomas J. Spear turned out to be, according to Jones, "devoid of principle, and reckless of character and everything else." While Jones quickly broke his association with Spear, he was too late to avoid lawsuits for debts. He lost everything in the ruined business.

Instead of turning to teaching as he had in the past, Jones returned to medicine. He hung his Latin diploma at No. 40 Canal Street and waited for patients. The cholera epidemic was over and people were again healthy. Few patients came. He was able to stick it out until the yellow fever season in the summer, when many people became ill.

Dr. Jones was succeeding reasonably well when he was struck down by yellow fever. He had to close his office for several weeks. By the time he was well enough to open his practice again, the yellow fever season was over. He had no patients and no money to tide him over. He had to look somewhere else to make a living.

During this time he met some Texans in New Orleans. Jeremiah Brown, captain of the *Sabine,* was in Texas trade. Brown was determined to convince Jones that Texas, a part of the Mexican Republic, was the ideal place for him. Texas was the land of opportunity, and Brazoria needed a physician. The doctor would be in great demand there, Brown told him.

Jones had heard things about Texas from non-Texans. The rumors were that the new frontier was a place for pirates and bandits. He wasn't interested in free land to become a farmer. He had been raised by a farmer and wanted nothing to do with that lifestyle. He had also been warned about "the unsettled political situation of the country."

Brown and his Texas friends argued with him. Professional people were moving to Texas: lawyers, a few teachers, ministers, and many politicians. But there were not enough physicians for the growing population. A practitioner could name his own fee and collect it, they said.

Jones took stock of his current situation. He had $32 in cash and $50 worth of medicine. He owed $2,000 and was facing a lawsuit. The fare to Texas was $15 if he slept on the deck of the *Sabine*. He decided to go to Texas and "take a look at the country and judge for himself," as Captain Brown urged him to do.

He was on the *Sabine* as it set sail for Texas on October 14, 1833. Unknown to him, he was sailing toward the greatest adventure of his life.

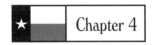

Chapter 4

A New Beginning in Texas

"[Stephen Fuller Austin] . . . . Twenty-seven years old; well educated for his day; experienced in public service and in business; patient; methodical; energetic; and fair-spoken. . . ."

Anson Jones was not the only young man to sail from New Orleans to Texas to change the course of history. Twelve years before Jones' arrival in Brazoria, Stephen F. Austin had left New Orleans to carry out his father's work in Texas.

Stephen's father, Moses Austin, had failed in several business ventures in Pennsylvania, Virginia, and Missouri. After the great depression of 1818–19, Moses had declared bankruptcy in St. Louis, Missouri. Stephen had managed Durham Hall Plantation and a lead mine for his father. During that time, Stephen served four years in the House of Representatives. He often questioned his business ability. He never questioned his political sense.

Moses Austin was impulsive, abrupt, and harsh. Unlike his father, Stephen was "patient, methodical, energetic, and fair-spoken." Moses said, "Texas is the place to begin again," and began planning for a

17

settlement in that untamed land. After much thought Stephen decided to help his father. He was twenty-seven years old and wanted to get on with his own life. They made plans for a colony of settlers in Texas. In November 1820, Moses headed for San Antonio de Bexar, which was then under Spanish rule. Stephen left for New Orleans to make arrangements for settlers who wanted to move to Texas.

Governor Antonio María Martínez was not kind to Moses and told him to leave Bexar at once. Baron de Bastrop, a friend of Moses from Louisiana, talked to Governor Martínez and presented Moses' application to settle families in Texas. After three days of consideration, Martínez approved the request and immediately sent it on to the commandant general of Eastern Interior Provinces of Spain. The land grant was approved in January 1821.

While Moses was petitioning for the land grant, Stephen was trying to make a place for himself. Politics and law were his interests. With a great deal of thought and planning, he began his law studies in New Orleans in January 1821. He became a clerk to Joseph H. Hawkins, in exchange for his room and board and being taught law by Hawkins. He earned extra money as the assistant editor of the *Louisiana Advertiser.*

Stephen had many dreams about his future. Those dreams ended abruptly when his mother wrote that his father was gravely ill. Moses had begged her from his sickbed to write to Stephen. He insisted that Stephen continue with his work for the Texas settlement. On June 18, 1821, Stephen left New Orleans to carry out his father's wishes. It was on his way to Texas that Stephen learned of his father's death.

Stephen met with Governor Martínez in San Antonio de Bexar. Martínez recognized him as heir to his father's commitments. Stephen agreed to follow the orders of the government of Spain. The settlement could bring provisions, tools, and farming equipment duty free through the port of San Bernard. Stephen was to be responsible for the good character of the immigrants. Until the government could organize the local administration, the settlers were under Stephen's rules. Stephen left for New Orleans to notify the public about this grant.

While Stephen organized his colony, Spain and Mexico were at war. The Mexican revolutionists swept the Spanish out of power. He had to stop his work and go to Mexico City for permission to continue his colony under Mexican rule.

The Mexican government was in turmoil. No one would take responsibility for passing the colonization law. For seven months Stephen F. Austin worked patiently to have his grant approved. When he left Mexico City on April 18, 1823, he had been gone a year.

The colonists had many problems in Stephen's absence. There were many rumors that Austin was dead and that land grants were denied. The Indians were hostile to the settlers. A severe drought destroyed the corn crops. The stories were greatly exaggerated in the United States. Immigration had almost stopped.

There were two settlements: one on the Colorado and one on the Brazos. Austin assured the settlers that their land grants were safe. The settlers pledged their allegiance to Mexico. They chose an *alcalde* (mayor), a captain, and a lieutenant. The *alcaldes* were given no guidelines or rules to follow. They lived in fear of offending some unfamiliar Mexican custom. In 1824, Austin wrote a set of "Instructions and regulations for the *Alcaldes*." By the end of that same year, 300 families were firmly established in Texas.

Austin applied for a second land grant to settle 300 more families. The government gave him approval for 500 families. The next few years were ones of rapid growth and prosperity among the settlers.

Austin was loyal to Mexico, but he wanted Texas to be an independent Mexican state. For that to happen the settlers had to adopt Mexican policy and law. The United States wanted to purchase Texas from Mexico. Austin did not want to annex Texas to the United States. Mexican officials became suspicious of the settlers and began questioning Austin's loyalty to Mexico.

Mexico passed a law on April 6, 1830, to stop the westward movement of people from the United States to Texas. Austin declared himself a Mexican citizen and urged the settlers to do the same. The settlers expressed their concerns about not having ministers, priests, or preachers. They wanted religious freedom, but Mexico recognized only the Catholic religion. Also, the Mexican government was trying to do away with slavery. The new colonization law of 1832 restricted slavery. Most colonists owned slaves.

The angry colonists held a convention in October 1832. Austin was elected president of the convention. The settlers wanted their own state government. They wanted Texas to be free of Coahuila. They wrote a petition to present to the Mexican government. But Santa Anna, temporary president of Mexico, would have been angered by the petition. He saw the convention as an act of independence. Austin calmed the group, and they did not send the petition.

The calm did not last long. The second convention met on April 1, 1833. William H. Wharton was elected president. Among the many newcomers to the delegation was Sam Houston, recently from Tennessee. Houston was in favor of annexing Texas to the United States. While there was some disagreement on that issue, the delegates were in general agreement on the convention's objective. Texans wanted the anti-immigration law repealed, and they wanted separate statehood.

General Houston submitted a state constitution, which was adopted by the convention against Austin's advice. The delegates begged Stephen to present it to Santa Anna in Mexico City. He did not want to do it, but he knew he had a better chance of succeeding than anyone else. With heavy heart, he left for Mexico City on April 23, 1833.

Both Stephen F. Austin and Anson Jones were trying to fulfill their fathers' dreams. Neither realized the impact they would make on the history of Texas because of those decisions.

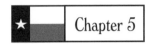

Chapter 5

The Colonists' Tension Grows

"[My] sole and exclusive object [was] to find a suitable field for the exercise of my profession . . . in an hour when there appeared little expectation of war. . . ."

Stephen F. Austin was in Mexico City when Anson Jones arrived in Velasco, Texas, on October 20, 1833. With his $17 and medicine worth $50, he made his way to Brazoria, the commercial center of the province. He took a look around and decided to book a return ticket on the *Sabine*. He remembered past failures and could only see one more in Texas.

Brazoria reminded him too much of his arrival in New Orleans, where he had found sickness and death. Austin had issued 1,055 land grants and the community around Brazoria was well-established. But the town had many problems. It was located on low ground, and the colonists often suffered from fever and chills (probably malaria). The Brazos River had overflowed in the summer of 1833, destroying crops and spreading sickness among the settlers. The cholera epidemic had reached Texas and taken its toll on the settlements along the river.

At Brazoria there had been eighty deaths, including the founder of the town, two physicians, the editor of the *Texas Gazette* (the only newspaper in the colony), and the owner of the boardinghouse.

When Jones reached Brazoria on November 1, the mark of death still hung over the town. The epidemic had passed, but Jones' skills and medicine were badly needed. By the time the *Sabine* was ready to return to New Orleans, local citizens had convinced Jones that he should stay and "give the place a fair trial."

He made friends with lawyer J. A. Wharton and other leaders of the town. Wharton took over the editorship of *Advocate of the People's Rights.* Within a month, he was advertising products and services, writing news articles, and voicing his opinion on current affairs. Frontier life was unknown to Jones. He watched in amazement as Brazoria began rapidly to recover its former enthusiasm and zest for life.

William Barret Travis was among the prominent citizens of Brazoria. He had come to Texas from South Carolina in 1831. Travis, a lawyer, divided his time between Brazoria and San Felipe de Austin, the unofficial capital of the American settlements. He wrote bills of sale, wills, deeds, titles, and occasionally acted as a special prosecutor. He accepted anything he could get in fees, as Jones would do when he set up practice. Travis was totally committed to his new country. When fifty representatives from the Texas colonies met in San Felipe on October 31, 1832, Travis was in the group. He wanted Texas to become independent of Mexico.

Jones learned how to be sociable, and he mixed

freely with the leaders of the community. He was not interested in politics. He had patients in both the War Party and Peace Party, as well as those who were neutral. He listened attentively to all opinions and said nothing. But he stored away information that would later be useful.

Jones had learned in Philadelphia that sick people prefer a physician whose first interest is medicine. He devoted all of his time to building a stable practice. He felt confident enough to take an apprentice to train in medicine. For the first time in his medical career, Jones was enjoying success.

The country was once again filling up with newcomers. Log houses began popping up in the clearings between the large plantations. Twenty families stopped in Brazoria, bringing its population back up to pre-cholera times. Immigrant trains passed through the town almost every day.

The spring sickly season began early in 1834. Dr. Jones was kept busy riding his forty-mile circuit night and day until September. He was attending a case of "bilious remittent fever" at the Phillips plantation when he fell ill to the same disease. He managed to return home, where he turned over his practice to his apprentice, James N. Berryman. After two months in bed, he thought he was going to die. He even made his will.

When he recovered, he decided he would take better care of himself. He had achieved status in the community and needed to live up to that standard. He rented and furnished a house and brought his unmarried sister Mary from New York to take care of it for him.

By the end of 1834, Jones had a practice worth $5,000. He believed that he could become "as wealthy as any man in Texas . . . from the practice of medicine . . . and the investments of its proceeds." He was respected as a practitioner of medicine and a tutor of medical apprentices. He let no outside interests distract him from his goal.

Wealth represented a way of life for him. He did not want to be a farmer, but he loved the luxurious plantation houses. He liked the cotton and cane fields tilled and harvested by slave labor. And he admired the plantation masters who wore suits imported from New York and hunted with hounds. Dr. Jones had never been entertained before in such luxury. He was determined to become "one of them" when he could afford it.

For the present time he continued to collect good fees in lands or chattel or mortgages. Sometimes, but not very often, he received Mexican or United States coins. His carefulness in money matters earned him the reputation of being frugal. He enjoyed the hospitality of the plantations without being expected to entertain in return. He learned all the manners of gracious living without the expense.

Unlike other immigrants to Texas, Jones was not interested in politics. He avoided political argument. His primary concern was winning friends and influencing them to call on him professionally.

The tranquility of Brazoria was gradually changing. When the cholera epidemic passed and the community began to recover, political tension grew. Stephen F. Austin was being held in a Mexico City prison. The colonists panicked. Austin wrote to them and advised them to remain calm. Fearing for his life, they did nothing to arouse suspicion from the Mexicans. But they continued to talk among themselves.

Juan N. Almonte visited Brazoria and other Brazos River towns in July 1834 to report to Mexican Vice-president Farias. Farias believed the colonists were ready to declare independence. Almonte reported that the Texans had been misunderstood. He believed the Texans would remain quiet if Mexico kept its politics stable.

There were disagreements between the Peace Party and the War Party. On November 8, 1834, an election was held to see if there should be another convention on November 15. Of the seventy-three citizens who voted, sixteen voted for the convention and fifty-seven voted against it.

Dr. Jones did not vote. He was still establishing his financial independence. It cost him little to live and he collected what was owed him. Seasonal illnesses, scarlet fever, and a local smallpox epidemic kept him constantly riding his circuit. But in the spring of 1835 he could no longer avoid becoming "an anxious observer of the political horizon of my adopted country." Revolution was under way in Texas.

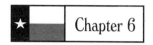

Chapter 6

The Revolution Calls

"This year (1835) the difficulties between Texas and Mexico assumed a character which made it quite apparent that a separation must take place. . . ."

Anson Jones was not quite ready to get involved in the revolution. There was no organization, no master plan. There was also mistrust among the Texans. Some questioned the motives of others. Communication was difficult. Many of the settlers were on isolated farms. What news they heard passed from one community to another in fragments. The individualism that brought men to Texas now brought conflict among them.

Dr. Jones attended to his professional business. His sister Mary ran his household efficiently. He sent for one of his cousins, Dr. Ira Jones of New York, to complete medical studies under his supervision. When Ira completed his apprenticeship and passed his exams, the two became partners under the shingle "Drs. Jones and Jones."

"I . . . attended closely to my professional duties and was this year eminently successful in business, though an anxious observer of the political horizon of my adopted country," Jones later wrote.

The "political horizon" grew nearer daily. Mexico re-established custom houses among the Texans at the beginning of 1835. The colonists had to pay duties (taxes) on everything brought into Texas. It was a violation of the Constitution of 1824. Captain Antonio Tenorio was put in charge at Anahuac and a deputy collector was stationed at Brazoria. All along the coast, garrisons concentrated on collecting duties and stopping any smuggling activity.

The Mexicans captured the Texas schooner *Martha*, which was loaded with supplies for the colonists. The colonists were angry. They burned some lumber that Tenorio had ordered at Anahuac. Tenorio threw some Texans in jail.

William Barret Travis reacted dramatically without thinking of the consequences. He quickly raised a small troop of men from the War Party in San Felipe and marched on Tenorio's headquarters. Tenorio surrendered without a fight on June 30, 1835, and agreed to leave the country. Instead of returning home a hero, Travis returned to criticism. The Peace Party saw it as an act of open rebellion.

Santa Anna decided to put a stop to the Texas uprising. He ordered his brother-in-law, General Martín Perfecto de Cós, to take personal command of the troops in Texas. The first action Cós took was to order the arrest of Travis, "Three-legged Willie" (R.M.) Williamson, and other prominent citizens. The citizens' own officials were ordered to make the arrests.

The Peace Party had supported Santa Anna until that time. Now they turned against him overnight. Public opinion changed. Cós moved his head-quarters to San Antonio de Bexar, where he hoped to enforce Mexican laws among the Texans.

By late summer of 1835, Anson Jones took his first steps toward joining the Texas revolution. John A. Wharton wrote a paper recommending the convening of delegates "instructed so that no party may rule, and that the people be fairly represented." Two copies were made to circulate among the colonists. Jones signed both.

"This document," he explained, "did not appear to embrace any *war* measure. There was a great division in the minds of the people. . . . I thought too few to divide, and, therefore, wished to bring about unison and concert of thought and action."

Stephen F. Austin returned from Mexico City after almost two years in prison. The convention had been planned but the delegates had not been chosen. He found a changed Texas, chaotic and disordered. Meetings were being held in all of the settlements. Conflicts were arising between those who wanted peace and those who wanted independence. War Party leaders and Peace Party friends hailed Austin as "the only physician that could correct the disorganized system and restore a healthy action to the body corporate."

All of the towns competed for the honor of being first to hear Stephen F. Austin speak. He was the leader of the Peace Party, which dominated San Felipe. He chose Brazoria, headquarters of the War Party, to make his first speech. He held peace or war within his hands.

"War," he declared, "is our only resource. There

is no other remedy but to defend our rights, ourselves and our country by force of arms."

Dr. Jones was in the Brazoria audience. He had never seen Stephen F. Austin before, but he had seen evidences of his wisdom and patience in Texas. Austin's tone and sound reasoning appealed to Jones. Jones' first step in joining the revolution was to sign the petition for a convention.

Three weeks after Austin's speech, Texans fought the first battle of the Texas Revolution. The settlers at Gonzales had a cannon. The Mexicans demanded they turn it over to their army. The Texans yelled, "Come and take it!" On October 2, 1835, the Mexican army attacked, but the Texans won the battle without losing a man.

The Texas army gathered at Gonzales and elected Stephen F. Austin commander-in-chief. The Texas army was not one to strike fear in the onlooker. The soldiers had no oaths to bind them to service. There was no uniform to give them identity. Each man furnished his own clothes, weapons, and horses.

Dr. Jones outfitted his cousin and partner, Ira Jones, with suitable clothes, weapon, and horse and released him to join the army. He also wrote letters of introduction to Old Ben Milam. The war was coming closer to Dr. Jones' household, and he was becoming anxious about his sister's safety.

Jones was not an elected delegate to the October 15 convention to be held at San Felipe. The convention had to be delayed because of the confusion of gathering an army. Many of the delegates had joined the army at Gonzales. Sam Houston came from Nacogdoches. He encouraged all of the delegates to return to San Felipe and hold the convention. Some of the delegates, including William Barret Travis, decided to remain with the army.

The convention met on November 3, 1835. Of the ninety-eight men elected, only fifty-eight attended this "Consultation of the Chosen Delegates of All Texas in General Convention Assembled." The war had been going on a month. The delegates would decide what the Texans were fighting for — independent rights as declared in the 1824 Constitution or independence from Mexico.

Although Jones had not been a candidate for the Consultation, he decided to observe what his elected delegates were doing. His trip to San Felipe was delayed by bad roads and stormy weather. By the time he got there, the Consultation was almost over. He was not happy with what he found.

There was criticism of Stephen F. Austin for not stopping the siege on San Antonio de Bexar and retreating to the east of the Colorado. Jones respected Austin and disliked Houston. He found "little dignity or patriotism" in the meeting.

Jones, who in the past had remained neutral and quiet, became very vocal. He thought all the talk about fighting for the principles of a dead constitution and re-establishing liberty in the Mexican republic was not only silly but dishonest.

"I took occasion . . . publicly to express my opinion of what I saw and heard, until my friend, Col. John A. Wharton . . . assured me my life was in danger," he wrote. "I returned to Brazoria, satisfied we were in a bad scrape, and that the best and only course was an unconditional declaration of independence."

In the "two or three days" that Jones spent in

San Felipe, he had met many of the politicians and the head of every government Texas was to have for ten years. The Consultation organized a provisional government, which was made up of a governor, lieutenant governor, and a council. His neighbor, Henry Smith, was elected governor. Sam Houston was elected commander-in-chief of the army. Stephen F. Austin, Branch T. Archer, and William H. Wharton were appointed commissioners to the United States. Their duty was to raise money and sympathy for the Texas cause.

Jones had no thoughts of a political career when he returned to Brazoria. But in December 1835, he decided to call a meeting of Brazoria County citizens at Columbia. "I drew up, offered, and advocated as chairman of the committee, resolutions in favor of a 'Declaration of Independence from Mexico' and calling a Convention of the people of Texas on the first Monday in March, 1836, to make the Declaration and to frame a Constitution," he reported.

There was a large attendance at the Columbia meeting. Jones did not trust a vote, so he passed around a petition to be signed. "Twenty to thirty" names were signed the first day. By the time the petition was printed, everyone who attended the meeting had signed it. The resolutions were published on Christmas Day.

Many years later Jones remarked that he took the first efficient step for the *independence* of Texas: "I had kept aloof and taken no part in bringing about or accelerating the public difficulties, but now they were upon us, I had no disposition to shrink from my duty or responsibility. The Crisis had come. . . ."

Dr. Jones no longer concentrated on his medical practice. He recognized "The Crisis" and responded with the responsibility of a Texas citizen.

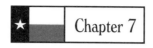

Chapter 7

The Storm Arrives

". . . evidence of an early and formidable invasion came with every breeze from the west."

The tranquil life in Texas that Dr. Jones had come to love was to be no more. He, Mary, and Ira celebrated New Year's Day, 1836, together. It was the last Jones family gathering. Mary would return to New York. Ira would join the army and prepare for battle. Anson himself was going to spend most of the year in military activity. Another more hectic career was about to begin for Dr. Anson Jones.

There was no mistaking the uneasiness and fear of what was to come as 1836 arrived. Santa Anna was furious about Cós surrendering Bexar to the Texans. He felt Cós had disgraced Mexico. There were evidences of a Mexican invasion in every town. Rumors spread as rapidly as the wind.

Colonel James C. Neill was in command at Bexar. Houston sent Bowie with thirty men to destroy the Alamo and abandon the fort. Neill and Bowie disobeyed their orders. They believed that

Bexar was the stronghold in Texas. In mid-January, when the Texans heard the Mexican army was moving toward Texas, Governor Smith sent Travis with a small group of Texas regulars to join Bowie at the Alamo.

The Texans knew that Santa Anna had raised an army and was moving toward Bexar. But they had underestimated Santa Anna's determination. They did not expect him to travel at such speed during the cold winter months. He did not have enough food for men or horses nor provisions for his troops. Santa Anna pushed on, leaving behind anyone who could not keep up.

Sam Houston ordered Jim Bowie and William Barret Travis to retreat from the Alamo. Bowie was in charge of the volunteers and Travis commanded the regulars. Houston told them to destroy anything the Mexicans might find useful. They were to take all military supplies to Gonzales. The men disobeyed Houston's orders and dug in to fight.

Travis sent his friend and messenger, James Butler Bonham, to Goliad to ask James Walker Fannin, commander of about 390 men, to come to their aid. Fannin made an ill-fated attempt to bring his command from Goliad. Lack of food, weapons, ammunition, clothing, and wagons doomed the trip from the beginning.

The provisional government that had been set up by the Consultation in November was falling apart. The governor was arguing with the council over who had the most power. If one gave an order, the other contradicted it. There was mass confusion among the ranks in the army.

A "Convention of the People of Texas at Washington-on-the-Brazos" was called before the provisional government fell apart completely. On February 1, Dr. Jones presided over Brazoria's polling place. Four delegates "clothed with ample, unlimited, or plenary powers" were elected representatives. Jones received five votes. He "declined all requests to become a candidate."

After the election, all normal routine of life disappeared. Around the middle of February, Jones sent his sister Mary back to New York and closed his house. He continued to care for his remaining patients while he began "to prepare for the storm."

On February 23, the Mexican army arrived in San Antonio de Bexar and began a thirteen-day siege on the Alamo the next day. It was also the day that William Barret Travis sent his message "To the People of Texas & All Americans in the World." He wrote in part: "I am besieged by a thousand or more Mexicans under Santa Anna . . . *I shall never surrender or retreat.*" He begged for someone "to come to our aid." He closed with the famous words: "Victory or Death."

The citizens of Bexar were taking their possessions and leaving Bexar as quickly as they could. Travis dispatched Bonham again to tell Fannin at Goliad to come with his troops. Bonham made the four-day round-trip needlessly. Fannin was not coming to help. When Bonham returned, he saw the blood-red flag still flying over San Fernando Cathedral. It meant "no quarter." There would be no mercy for the Texans.

The "Convention of the People of Texas at Washington-on-the Brazos" met on March 1. They worked all night to draft a statement of independence. George Childress, who wrote the statement, modeled it after America's Declaration of Independence written by Thomas Jefferson in 1776.

Texas was declared an independent republic on March 2, 1836.

The commission hurriedly put together a constitution. Again, this was modeled after those of the United States and some Southern states. The president could serve only three years. He could not succeed himself nor could he lead an army in the field without the consent of Congress. No clergyman of any faith could hold an office. Each family head in Texas was entitled to a league and one labor (4,605 acres) of land. Slavery was legalized, but slave-running was against the law.

They selected officers to run the Republic only for the duration of the war (an interim government). David G. Burnet became acting president, with Lorenzo de Zavala as vice-president. Thomas Rusk was elected secretary of war, and Sam Houston was re-elected commander-in-chief of the army. This commission gave him more power than he had before. He now commanded all armed men in Texas, regular and volunteer.

Before the convention adjourned, they received horrifying news. The Alamo had fallen on March 6, 1836. One hundred and ninety defenders were killed in the battle and placed in a heap on a funeral pyre. They were shown "no quarter." Their bodies were burned.

The Runaway Scrape, which had begun as early

as the middle of January, grew quickly after the fall of the Alamo. People all over Texas left everything behind and made their way toward safety. When Sam Houston arrived in Gonzales on March 11, the Runaway Scrape had become a panic run eastward to escape the angry Mexican army. Houston ordered Fannin at Goliad to blow up the fortress and retreat. He wanted the whole Texas army together for strength.

Anson Jones heard nothing but bad news as travelers passed through Brazoria. Some were recruits going westward trying to find some part of the Texas army. Settlers were going eastward in the Runaway Scrape. The citizens of Brazoria were closing their houses and "taking the Sabine chute," a navigable river, moving as fast as possible toward the United States border.

News reached Brazoria that the Alamo had fallen. The "storm" Jones had anticipated had arrived. "An invaded, unarmed, unprovided country, without an army to oppose invaders and without money to raise one" was in a state of panic and confusion.

Brazorians joined the Runaways in great numbers, leaving houses full of personal possessions. Jones left his business and medical practice with his cousin Ira. He instructed Ira that if Brazoria had to be abandoned, Ira was to join him in the army. Anson Jones appeared before the Land Board on March 16 to claim a league and a labor of land. He left on March 19 with other Brazorians to find Sam Houston's army. He was unconditionally committed to Texas independence.

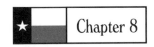

Chapter 8

Private Anson Jones

"In March came the news of the fall and massacre of the Alamo, and I immediately enlisted as a volunteer private soldier in Capt. Calder's company, 2d Regiment infantry...."

D r. Anson Jones found the army on March 24 at Beason's Ferry on the Colorado (near present Columbus). Some said Houston's troops numbered more than 1,200. Others said there were 1,800 men, but no one knew exactly. Jones enlisted as a private in Captain Robert J. Calder's infantry company. On the day Jones arrived, Houston sent a message back to Brazoria: "Our Army will never leave the Colorado, but go on westward."

Without explaining why, Houston moved eastward the next day. The troops were disgusted by the retreat. More than half of his men quit the army. Volunteers on their way to join the army turned around and fled eastward with their families. The Runaway Scrape had gained momentum. President Burnet said Texas was "a moving mass of fugitives."

Houston had ordered Colonel Fannin to destroy La Bahia and retreat from Goliad. Instead of retreating, Fannin sent one-third of his troops to help the Anglo settlers leave the region. Fannin tried to leave on March 19, but it was too late. He and his men were surrounded by General Urea's army and forced to surrender at the battle of Coleto.

On Palm Sunday, March 27, 1836, Colonel James Walker Fannin and his command, consisting of 390 Americans, were massacred at Goliad.

Stories of the Alamo and Goliad and the army's retreat struck horror in the hearts of all Texans. On the last day of March "the unruly Texas army reached Groce's Retreat on the Brazos." They were in a state of mutiny. General Houston's answer to that was stricter discipline.

Private Anson Jones was assigned judge advocate general of a court-martial that considered cases of insubordination. One soldier, "a hardened villain," was sentenced to be shot.

Robert Hancock Hunter wrote of the account:

The hole Army was marched out to the ground, the grave was dug & a coffin was there, & the Army was formed in a half circle, a round grave. The man was blindfolded, & made to kneel on the ground by the coffin, & there [were] 12 men to shoot him, the officer gave command. He said present arms, take ame. Just at that moment, Colonel Hockley was coming in a lope from camp, hollowing, halt, halt, halt, & the oficer said order arms. Colonel Hockley rode up and said Lieutenant here is repreave.

This disciplinary action had little effect because most of the men felt the condemned man deserved to die anyway. Houston's real problems were average

41

citizens who believed they were better soldiers than their general.

Santa Anna was not having the morale problem that Houston was having. Santa Anna felt confident that at Bexar and Goliad the Texas rebellion had been stopped. He believed the entire Texian army was destroyed, and so he decided to return to Mexico. His officers talked him out of it. They wanted revenge. They wanted to exterminate all rebels so there would be no more uprising from the Anglos.

Santa Anna divided his troops into five divisions under different commands. The troop commanders' orders were to burn every town, plantation or dwelling in their paths.

President Burnet moved the seat of government to Harrisburg on Buffalo Bayou, near Galveston Bay. He wrote to Sam Houston that "the enemy are laughing you to scorn. You must fight them. You must retreat no farther. The country expects you to fight. The salvation of the country depends on you doing so."

While the army was camped in the Brazos swamp, an epidemic of dysentery broke out and "nearly every tenth man had measles." A medical corps was organized and manned by enlisted doctors. Private Anson Jones agreed to be "surgeon to the 2d Regiment." He made it conditional in that he "should be permitted to resign so soon as the necessity of my acceptance of the place should cease." Jones later remarked that "there was not a single death in the 2d Regiment from the time I was appointed, until the battle on the 21st of April."

Private Jones saw little of General Houston until both were invited to a dinner party at the Groce plantation. Houston asked Jones in private what he thought about the way things were going. Jones told him, "The men [are] deserting and if the retreating policy [is] continued much longer, [you] will be pretty much alone."

Houston told Jones that he suspected a "traitor" among the officers in the army. He asked Jones if he would guess who it might be. Jones immediately answered, "It is one of your volunteer aids, Col. Perry." Jones told Houston that he thought Perry was a "reckless fool," but that Perry was just one example of the many who were dissatisfied in the camp. Houston seemed thoughtful and let the matter drop. While Jones had his attention, he added with earnest hope that Houston's next move would be *toward* the enemy.

General Houston spent the weeks on the Brazos drilling and training his army, which had grown to 1,400 men. No one except Houston and a few of his officers had ever fought in formal warfare. He knew they did not stand a chance against Santa Anna's trained and disciplined troops without a good plan.

Houston did not follow Jones' advice. When the army resumed its march, it moved eastward. They pitched their camp opposite the smoking ruins of Harrisburg before noon on April 18. There they captured a Mexican messenger, and Houston learned that Santa Anna was at the San Jacinto River, less than one day's march to the east. The captured Mexican courier's saddlebags had "belonged to Travis . . . had his name upon them." As word spread among the troops, their anger and determination to fight the Mexicans grew.

The next morning Houston wrote an official letter of intentions and delivered it in person to Rusk, the secretary of war. He stated: "This morning we are in preparation to meet Santa Anna . . . . We go to conquer. It is wisdom growing out of necessity . . . . My country will do justice to those who serve her."

Houston and Rusk addressed the soldiers. "The army will cross, and we will meet the enemy," Houston said. He called upon all cowards to fall out. He ended with a battle cry: "Remember the Alamo! Remember La Bahia!"

The troops echoed his cry. "Remember the Alamo! Remember La Bahia!"

More than a hundred soldiers were sick with measles and diarrhea. They were left in Harrisburg under guard. Dr. Jones was one of the surgeons assigned to stay there. The hospital surgeon, Dr. Phelps, was also directed to take care of them.

For the first time since the army gathered, they were marching toward the enemy instead of away from them. Private Jones decided to disobey the order. "[He] . . . attended to [his] daily routine, handed over [his] sick to the hospital surgeon, and joined the army . . . about sundown and proceeded with it to Lynchburg." He did not want his medical duties to interfere with the duties of his combat rank.

The army marched until two o'clock the next morning. After an hour's rest, they started again. At six they stopped for a quick breakfast. One of the surgeons wrote about the experience:

Our guns were stacked, and three cows that happened to be near by, were shot down and im-

44

mediately large numbers started off for wood to kindle fires. The surgeons' mess was the third fire kindled. A pot of brackish water with a handful of half-pounded coffee thrown in was ready to boil, when Dr. Booker came up with a dozen eggs, which were at once put in the pot of coffee to boil.

At this moment the spies were coming up in a gallop, and the word was given: "To arms, to your arms!" The eggs were taken out, and each one drinks his small share of the hot boiling coffee the best way he could; but when the eggs were found to contain chickens, I surrendered my share to others, who finding them well cooked, swallowed them quickly, when each seized his rifle and hastened to his post, leaving some fifty fires just kindled.

Around midmorning on April 20, the Texans were near Lynch's Ferry when they saw Santa Anna's guard approaching. They fell back about one-half mile to a liveoak grove on the plain of San Jacinto.

The Mexicans camped near the south edge of the prairie. They had lunch and then attacked the Texans' camp with grapeshot from their six-pounder. The Texans had a cannon named "Twin Sisters," a gift of Cincinnati, Ohio. They answered the Mexicans by shooting broken horseshoes toward their camp.

About four o'clock in the afternoon, Sidney Sherman called for volunteers to capture the Mexican cannon. Sixty-eight Texans found horses and galloped toward the enemy. Four companies of Mexican infantry came filing out near the cannon. The Texans had driven their cavalry almost back to the cannon when the Mexican trumpet sounded "no quarter." The Texans were exposed to the cavalry, the artillery, and 200 infantry. When the Texas infantry did not come to their rescue, the volunteer group reluctantly retreated.

Surgeon General Ewing, Surgeon Jones of the Second Regiment, and Surgeon Nicholas D. Labadie examined the wounded. The medical corps took over Vice-president Zavala's house across the bayou for a field hospital. Patients were taken there.

The Texans rested very little during the night. They were excited about being so close to the Mexicans. They were also unhappy that Houston had not taken part in the skirmish that afternoon. No food had been provided. They ate what scraps of food they had in their pockets. They were uncertain what Houston planned to do. The camp was in an uproar.

The night guard was doubled and the men finally settled down for a few hours of uneasy rest. Early the next morning, word began spreading that while the Texans sat and waited, the Mexican army had doubled in number. Around midmorning Colonel Wharton went through the camps, slapping his hands together and saying, "Boys, there is no other word today but fight, fight! Now is the time!"

Houston became angry with Wharton and held a war council at noon on April 21. He planned to attack on the morning of April 22. His officers agreed with him. The men under their command disagreed. They were rebellious and impatient to fight. They voted company by company to attack immediately.

Houston was outvoted. He sent Deaf Smith and a few trusted men to destroy Vince's Bridge across the Brazos. It cut off the Mexican retreat, but it also trapped the Texans. They would either win or be exterminated. For the first time since the war began, the Texas army was united. Each company was given an assignment.

As the lines of attack were forming, the medical corps realized they had not been assigned specific stations. None of the doctors had been in combat before. There was no time for anyone to tell them what was customary. They decided "to follow the line, and fight with our arms as circumstances might dictate." Private Jones, surgeon of Sherman's regiment, was joined by Surgeon Labadie as the first shots were fired.

At three o'clock Houston had his attack in place. Sixty horsemen were mounted on the right under the command of Mirabeau Buonaparte Lamar. Colonel Henry Millard directed two small companies of the Texas Regular Army. The Twin Sisters were manned by the regular infantry. Then came Burleson's First Regiment, followed by Moseley Baker's riflemen and backed up with Sidney Sherman's Kentucky volunteers.

Houston formed a line of infantry, one man deep. The Texans had no bayonets for direct combat. They carried rifles, tomahawks, and bowie knives. In the center of the line the Republic's flag blew in the wind: plain white silk with five-pointed azure star and the motto *Ubi Libertas Habitat Ibi Nostra Patria Est* — "Where liberty lives, there is our homeland." General Sam Houston rode his huge white stallion, Saracen, beside the flag.

Four men volunteered to provide field music for the march. They did not know any military music, so Houston told them to strike up "Come to the Bower," a popular but bawdy song of the day. Houston drew his sword, the music began, and the troops' voices sounded across the prairie.

The enemy was unprepared for the afternoon attack. Santa Anna and most of his men were in their tents taking *siestas*. There were no guards or sentries watching the Texas camp. Some of the Mexicans were leading their horses to water. Others were sitting around, paying little attention to their surroundings.

The Texans rushed the camp, yelling, "Remember the Alamo! Remember Goliad!" Houston's favorite horse, Saracen, was shot and killed. He grabbed another mount from an aide and continued in battle. His second horse was shot from beneath him, and this time he was hit in the ankle with a copper musket ball.

"Remember the Alamo! Remember Goliad!" reverberated through the dusty, smoke-filled air. The Texans' shouts drowned out the cries of Santa Anna's terrified army.

The battle lasted only eighteen minutes. The Mexicans fired their cannon three times. The confused army stopped fighting. Some threw down their arms and begged for mercy. Some fled the scene. The Texans showed "no quarter" in revenge for the Battle of the Alamo and the Goliad massacre. Six hundred and thirty Mexicans were killed. Another 600, including 200 wounded, were taken prisoners. They sat on the ground, dazed by the horror of the battle.

Two Texans were killed in action and about thirty wounded, seven of whom died later. The San Jacinto deaths added to almost 600 who had died at the Alamo and Goliad. It was a heavy price that Texans paid for their independence.

In the aftermath of the attack, Private Anson Jones stumbled across two folio books on the battlefield. They were important-looking Spanish manuscripts. He carefully preserved them to examine later. He discovered that he had Colonel Juan N. Almonte's "Private Journal of the Texas Campaign" and his general order book. He later sent it to the *New York Herald,* but at that time he had no interest in becoming a historian. He had too many wounded men who needed his attention.

The Doctor Joins Congress

*"I participated in the battle of San Jacinto . . .
and that night was occupied the entire time,
until sunrise the next morning, in assisting
to dress the wounds received on the field. . . . "*

The wounded Texans were taken to General Zavala's house, which was still being used as the field hospital. Twenty-three of them lay on the floor because there were no beds or cots. Their wounds were dressed with torn bedsheets until they were all used.

Dr. Jones attended Dr. Mottley, who had been fatally wounded. He asked Dr. Labadie to assist him, but there was nothing either could do. Dr. Mottley had been shot through the abdomen and mercifully died quickly. Jones grieved his friend's death while trying to save others.

The day after the Battle of San Jacinto, Santa Anna and Cós were recognized and brought to General Houston. Santa Anna had been in his tent in his underwear when the Texans attacked. He dressed in a private soldier's gray trousers and tried to slip away. When he was caught and returned to camp, the Mexican soldiers all treated him with such authority and respect that it gave away his identity.

Houston, who was suffering from his leg wound, had Santa Anna's tent set up next to his and posted guards around it. For several days the two generals bargained over the results of the battle. The Mexican president wanted to be released immediately to return home. Houston refused until Santa Anna agreed to send orders to all of his troops in Texas to stop all aggression against the Texans.

By May 5, all of the government officials had reached San Jacinto to take charge of the civil and military situation. Houston's wound grew worse from neglect. The surgeon general prescribed an operation in New Orleans. Private Jones put his cousin Ira in charge of the health of the Second Regiment when President Burnet appointed him to apothecary general. Under his new title, Anson Jones accompanied Houston and Santa Anna to Galveston.

Apothecary General Jones went on to Velasco to wait until the treasury could find a hundred dollars for his official trip to New Orleans. Before the end of May, he reached New Orleans as a buyer for the medical corps of the Texas army. He was authorized to purchase necessary medical supplies for the new independent nation.

Dr. Jones arrived in New Orleans too late to take part in the initial parties celebrating Texas' victory and Houston's triumphant arrival. He did visit Jeremiah Brown, who had captured the American brig *Pocket* on its way to Mexico with a cargo of war material. This was the same Jerry Brown who, less than three years earlier, had persuaded Jones there might be a place for him in Texas.

Jones returned to his home in Brazoria in mid-summer of 1836 to take up his private life. The town had suffered during war. Many of the Brazorians had fled in the Runaway Scrape. Gradually, those who had been with the army or had "taken the Sabine chute" returned. It was months before normal activity was restored. Brazoria never recaptured its character of a solid community. Its days of greatness had passed.

Beyond the town, other things had changed. Anything portable that could be moved had been taken. Families returned to find their farmhouses stripped bare. Crops were overgrown with weeds. Fences and barns were burned to the ground. Some chose not to start over and moved to towns. Houston was a growing city, and many families moved there to begin again.

Texas was in a state of confusion and unhappiness. The temporary capital had been moved to Columbia. Government officials were resigning their posts because of political conflict. President Burnet scheduled the first general election for the first Monday in September 1836. Texans were asked to vote on the new Constitution and to express their opinions about annexation to the United States.

Voters were not focused on either of those issues. They were more interested in who was going to be elected president, vice-president, senators, and congressmen. Sam Houston and Stephen F. Austin were candidates for president. Austin had stood by the colonists and served them faithfully for years. But Houston was the hero of the moment. When the votes were counted, General Sam Houston won the presidency by a great majority vote.

President-elect Houston asked Austin to become secretary of state. Austin declined but accepted an appointment to the Senate, where he served until his death on December 27, 1836.

Anson Jones had listened closely to the bitter political discussions but took no part in the campaign. He never said for whom he voted. He spent his time visiting old friends along the Brazos and San Bernard rivers. He was at William A. Wharton's Eagle Plantation when he fell ill with dysentery. It took him two months to recover.

While he was on Eagle Island recovering, his cousin Ira returned to Brazoria. Before Anson Jones could return, Ira fell ill and died. When Anson finally arrived in Brazoria, he found his house had been broken into. Everything including saddles, bridles, and blankets had been stolen. His desk had been robbed of all his money. He wrote in his autobiography:

> Two lawyers had "squatted" in one room of my office and I was unable to get them out for several weeks; when I succeeded it produced a "challenge" from my friend the Chief Justice J. Collinsworth, which I accepted, to fight with pistols at ten steps. It was, however, settled, his object having been to "bluff," which, when he found out it would not succeed, he got his friend T.F. McKinney to get him out of the scrape.

At nearby Columbia the newly elected officials set to work. The temporary capital resembled more of a campground than a seat of government. The statesmen met in barn-like buildings and sat on rickety, wooden benches. Some slept rolled up in their blankets under trees.

Columbia was ten miles from Brazoria. Dr. Jones had ridden that circuit for three years and began to ride it again. Never before had he watched so closely the legislative and executive process. He became aware of the keenness of his own political judgments. He studied proposed legislation as carefully as men who sat in Congress. He began to listen to people who wanted him to become a candidate for Congress.

Dr. Anson Jones had changed dramatically from the time he arrived in Texas. He now reflected on the state of the nation as he rode between the plantations of his patients. He discussed public questions in such a reasonable way that other men began thinking of him as a potential statesman.

When Senator Collingsworth from Brazoria resigned from Congress to become chief justice of the Republic, the *Telegraph and Texas Register* listed Dr. Anson Jones as a candidate to replace him. A startled Dr. Jones wrote the editors to explain that it was a misunderstanding "of some remarks made by me on the subject of the pending election . . . . However grateful I might be, under other circumstances, for the suffrages of my fellow citizens . . . I am not now a candidate for them."

Jones was trying to convince himself that he wanted no public office. He wanted nothing more than a successful medical practice, which he had. His withdrawal from a race that he had not entered actually committed him to politics. He reviewed more closely the actions of the first Congress and questioned some of its acts, especially the charter it had granted to the Texas Railroad, Navigation and Banking Company.

Those who supported the charter were interested in its economic impact on themselves. The charter was rushed through Congress and signed by President Houston. Dr. Jones decided that it was time for disinterested men to stop agreements between spectators and government that the Texas Railroad, Navigation and Banking Company charter symbolized.

Jones' friends again urged him to run for Congress, and this time he agreed to do it. He wanted to see Texas "prosperous and successful." He felt "the first Congress of Texas had committed the most woful [sic] blunders, and there had been much reckless and interested legislation."

He was very upset over the charter granted to the Texas Railroad, Navigation and Banking Company. He thought moving the capital of Texas to Houston was a mistake and the selling of Galveston Island a disgrace. He believed that "these three acts constituted a perfect 'selling out' of Texas to a few individuals, or at least, of everything that was available in 1836."

There was great opposition to the monopoly of the Banking Company policies. Texans did not understand how it could be anything but bad news for individuals. They feared their mortgages and currency would become worthless. Dr. Anson Jones led the opposition in Brazoria County.

Supporters of the charter turned against him. He wrote an article under the name of "Franklin" and sent it to the editor of the *Matagorda Bulletin*. He pointed with pride to honorable Texans outside of Congress. He was alarmed at the "monster Congress had created to enslave them." The article stated: "Fellow citizens! this institution . . . will destroy, in ten thousand ways, *the liberties of your country.*"

Before the article was published on August 19, 1837, the *Houston Telegraph* had announced Jones' candidacy for Congress. The article, which was widely circulated, asked, "Was it for this you fought and bled at Velasco, at Goliad, at Conception, at San Antonio, and at San Jacinto?" His closing statement challenged, "Let your consciences answer these questions, and let the response be given at the polls . . . September 4th, when you will be called upon to choose between the advocates and the opposers of this institution."

Dr. Anson Jones was elected to the Second Congress. His political career had begun.

Chapter 10

A Proposal of Marriage

"I again returned to Houston and became engaged to be married to . . . Mrs. Mary McCrory."

Houston, the crowded, loud, and rowdy new city, was the seventh capital of Texas in its short fourteen months of independence. Dr. Jones and Patrick Churchill Jack were representatives of Brazoria County when the Second Congress convened on September 25, 1837. It didn't take Jones long to understand that nothing was done quickly in Congress. He could not achieve his purpose instantly.

Jones was a methodical, reasonable man. He had learned from his past experiences that things had to be done in order. He approached his new job as a physician would: first diagnose the problem and then try to find a cure.

Without intending to do so, Jones laid the foundation for a career that took all his energies for the next ten years. He believed at the time that he would quit politics at the end of his first term in office.

57

Jones believed the country was in "a bad scrape." He wanted to do something to correct the mistakes that had been made. Legislation had created a mess that could not be cleared up quickly. For every piece of bad legislation that had been passed, the Second Congress had to go through a lengthy process to correct it. The end of one active phase sent him on to tackle another problem. He soon forgot the days when his major concerns were those of a county physician.

Jones was present at the opening session of the Second Congress, although most of the representatives did not appear until the second day. He called for the proclamation that called Congress together, and he counted ballots for the Speaker of the House. He also escorted the new Speaker to the podium. Jones served as chairman of the House committee to inform President Sam Houston that the Congress was ready to receive him.

During Jones' service in the House he served on many committees. He was usually on the arrangements committee, which escorted and introduced dignitaries. He wrote the rules for the reception of non-members. "Mr. Jones of B." (as he is referred to in records because there was a "Mr. Jones of A.") was a respected worker on the floor and in committees. He became chairman of the committee on privileges and elections, of the ways and means committee, and of the committee on foreign relations.

Mr. Jones of B. was also on special assignments. One was to a select committee to consider repeal of the Texas Railroad, Navigation and Banking charter. Not for the first nor last time, Jones was in an unhappy situation. He felt it was as unconstitutional to repeal the charter as it had been for the First Congress to approve it. He addressed the House and recommended the matter to be turned over to the Supreme Court. "I want to see the company tried and executed, not murdered!" he declared.

The corporation had not destroyed the country as Jones had feared. The death of the bank was not due to anything that Jones or the Republic of Texas did. The company could not raise enough money in stocks to issue currency. Most Texans had little money in coins, and paper money was worthless. They had nothing to invest. When Jones left Congress, the Texas Railroad, Navigation and Banking Company was dead.

Jones' next issue was public finance after he became aware of the plight of Texas currency. Panic had begun in the United States over the problems of the banking industry in 1837. The effects carried over to Texas. If United States currency was at risk, how could Texas repay its debts? If the Republic could not guarantee payment, it could not borrow needed money to operate.

One settler commented, "Things were so bad, a fellow could light his cigar with a $10 note and not be out ten cents."

A mass meeting was held in Houston to consider the financial problems of the Republic. Jones wrote the declaration of policy that was adopted.

"Treasury drafts," he declared, "if issued within the range of actual resources, will be safe, valid, secure, and convenient." The only way out for Texans was to accept no currency except that issued by the Republic of Texas.

Newspapers throughout the Republic published Jones' policy, and he became known as an authority on public finance. He was soon studying and interpreting the financial reports of the secretary of treasury for other members of the House. He suggested that a loan of $5 million be sought in London and Paris as well as in Washington. He had many recommendations for changes and improvements in Texas finance.

Before Anson Jones became a member of the House, he had presented a petition to Congress for medical legislation. He drafted the first request for governmental regulation of the practice of healing in the Republic of Texas. In June 1837, Jones had petitioned the First Congress to act quickly to protect the Texans against untrained physicians. He warned that there were too many "Individuals assuming Physicians who . . . have neither graduated or been licensed." He asked that a Medical Society or Board of Medical Censors be created. He wanted Congress to pass a bill regulating fees "and all other matters relating to the Medical Profession."

Medical lobbyists wrote a bill for Congress that would have created a Medical Board. Anson Jones was one of the seven physicians recommended for the board. However, the bill died before the First Congress adjourned.

Newspapers took up the issue and stirred up the population. The Second Congress passed the medical bill but required censors or examiners to be elected by Congress. Eleven respected physicians were elected to regulate the medical profession in Texas.

Another problem of the Republic that interested

Jones was public education. As the only congressman who had graduated from college, he was concerned that there were no state-supported schools in
Texas. One of the Texans' criticisms of Mexico was
that there were no schools.

The Texas Constitution made it a duty of Congress to provide schools as soon as possible. The
First Congress did not discuss the issue. During the
Second Congress, Congressman Douglass of Nacogdoches moved to begin public education at the top
with the establishment of the University of Texas.
Jones was opposed because he felt an institution of
higher learning could not survive without students
with a proper foundation. The children of Texas, like
the dozen or so at his boardinghouse who were being
taught by their older sister Mary, might someday
need a university, he agreed. But in 1837 they
needed to learn their ABCs and numbers.

Jones recommended that Congress establish a
general and uniform system of education. He proposed and won approval for land to be set aside for a
university at the *permanent* seat of government.
(The capital kept moving from one place to another.)
To Jones' disgust, another congressman got both
proposals referred to the judiciary committee. They
remained there to die when the Second Congress adjourned. But Jones noted in his diary: "W.H. Wharton has promised me to bring the matter up again
next session."

For the present time he would concentrate on
Mary Smith McCrory, schoolmistress to her dozen or
so brothers and sisters in the Woodruff household
where he was boarding.

Congressman Jones found a clean room, good

food, and an orderly existence at the Woodruffs. Still, he missed the luxury and hospitality of the Brazos and San Bernard plantations. More than that, he missed the quiet house and comforts his sister had provided for him at Brazoria. For a year and a half he had been without a home base. He was ready for another home of his own.

Young and sad Mary Smith McCrory, in her widow's mourning clothes, caught his eye. Mary was born in Lawrence, Arkansas, on July 24, 1819. She was twenty-one years younger than Congressman Jones, but the age difference was unimportant to them. Mary had a remarkable mind and memory. She was well-educated for a young woman in the early 1800s. She was also very pretty.

Mary's mother, Sarah Pevehouse Smith, had been widowed before she left Arkansas to move to Texas in 1834. Gray-eyed Mary was fourteen years old and already taking care of her four brothers and sisters. When her mother homesteaded a farm in Brazoria County, Mary became the homemaker.

The Smiths' farm was next to John Woodruff's land. John admired Sarah Smith's spunk in claiming a homestead with no man to help. John was a widower with six children. In October 1835, the Woodruffs and Smiths joined households.

Mary was sixteen and the oldest child of both households. She continued to run the house and to be governess to all of the children. If it was a lot of work, Mary never complained. She was happy with her new life.

Mary was aware of unrest among the settlers. She had listened to discussions about the fate of

Texas, but the Woodruffs were not involved. They were concentrating on farming and raising their large brood of children. Then the dreaded alarm sounded when Santa Anna and his troops camped three miles away. The Mexicans were slaying and destroying all in their paths. Mary and her mother stayed up all night preparing for the family to flee.

The Woodruff family was luckier than some settlers. They had a covered cart and a team of oxen. The women chose carefully what to take: bed coverings, ticking slips to fill with grass or corn shucks for their mattresses, a few cooking utensils, clothing, bacon, coffee, corn, and a steel mill for grinding. At early light the large family slipped quietly from their homestead, leaving valuable possessions behind. They moved eastward as part of the Runaway Scrape.

Thirty families camped on Clear Creek, hiding from the Mexicans. They posted guards to watch for Indians as well as the Mexicans. The Woodruffs' steel mill was the only one in the camp and was kept busy grinding every day. Mary was the unofficial "school marm." She taught her brothers and sisters along with any other children who wanted to learn their ABCs.

After the Battle of San Jacinto and the capture of Santa Anna, the Woodruff family returned home. They found that everything had been destroyed or carried away. Fences had been knocked down. Barns and outhouses had been burned to the ground. Their crops had been trampled into the ground. There was nothing left.

John and Sarah Woodruff decided to go to Houston, the new capital, to start again. When they arrived, there were only two buildings in town and a lot of prairie land, but no houses. They set up tents next to the old San Felipe Cemetery on the bank of Buffalo Bayou and began building a house.

"Woodruff's near the old grave yard" became a stopping place for travelers to the new city. To their already large family, John and Sarah added paying guests. The house was crowded and uncomfortable, but it did have a roof to dry-out under. Eighteen-year-old Mary was general manager of the growing household. John and Sarah gradually added four more children to their original eleven.

Mary was self-confident, sincere, and pretty. Although modest, she had grown up in pioneer times in Arkansas and Texas and could work as hard as a man.

There were more bachelors in Houston than there were women to marry them. Hugh McCrory, a twenty-seven-year-old Kentuckian, was an eligible bachelor looking for a wife. He found Mary Smith. They were married on July 23, 1837, and were very happy. They lived with the Woodruffs while they saved household supplies for their own home. Hugh's business prospered. He became a municipal official. Then, on September 13, less than two months after their wedding, Hugh died suddenly.

Mary dressed in her mother's black dress for her year of mourning. She quietly and sadly continued in her role of general manager of the Woodruff household. At her stepfather's house she listened, as she passed platters of buffalo meat and fluffy biscuits, to the conversations of the men who were making history.

Twelve days after Hugh McCrory's death, Anson Jones arrived in Houston. He took a room at Woodruff's boardinghouse. He was not a stranger to Mary. She had heard of him in Brazoria when she was a little girl. Now she saw him every day and listened as he discussed problems of state.

Jones was kind, considerate, and tactful. He was not a rough frontiersman. He was a gentle physician. He respected that she was in mourning for her recently lost husband. Mary was the most attractive young widow he knew. He began to flirt with her slowly, giving her time to adjust to her grief.

Mary began doing small favors for the congressman. She sewed on lost buttons and repaired frayed cuffs. There was an increasing awareness between them as the months slipped by. But Jones knew that Mary's year of mourning must pass before he could openly court her.

When spring came, a brightness replaced the sadness in Mary's beautiful gray eyes. She put aside her widow's black garments. She was once again a radiant and pretty young woman. Anson Jones wasted no time in proposing. When Congress adjourned in May 1838, Mary had said, "Yes."

They planned to be married in June. Private citizen Dr. Anson Jones left for Brazoria to set up a home for his future bride.

Chapter 11

Marriage Must Wait

"In consequence of accepting this appointment, the marriage arrangement was postponed . . . ."

D r. Anson Jones discarded his congressman's duties as one would an empty dinner plate. He had his fill and now would move on to his "other" life. He left Houston with a happy heart. Mary and he were to be married soon. He needed to make arrangements for their homecoming.

He arrived in Brazoria to find a smaller town than when he left before the Battle of San Jacinto. It would never be the bustling city that Houston was becoming, but he liked the peaceful, contented atmosphere. He and Mary could live there without political or financial worries.

He busily dusted his bottles, made lists of supplies to be ordered from Houston or New Orleans, and got his office in order. He secretly told a few close friends that the house he was fixing up would soon be run by Mary — not his sister Mary but his wife. He went about town telling people that his medical practice would soon be open for business.

Dr. Jones' happy activities were interrupted when a messenger from General Sam Houston arrived. President Houston wrote: "I have resolved to appoint you the agent from this Government, for the purpose of procuring a navy in the United States." Jones left Brazoria and returned to the capital. President Houston had changed his mind. He now wanted Jones to become minister plenipotentiary to the United States. He would have full power and authority to represent the Republic in Washington.

At first Jones declined the offer. He didn't want to postpone his marriage and be away from Mary a whole year. But Houston pressured him to accept and leave for Washington by July 8. Finally, on June 22, he agreed to go. He and Mary decided to wait until he returned from Washington to be married. She would continue living with the Woodruffs until he came for her. He knew he was taking a risk that Mary would find someone else. She was young and pretty and would be lonely.

Before Minister Jones left Houston, he became very ill. One treatment for a fever such as he had was "to bleed" the person. Leeches, blood-sucking worms that live in water, were placed on the sick person's body to suck out the sick blood. During Jones' illness a "Mr. La Branche called to see [him] twice and assisted in bleeding [him]." It took almost a month for Jones to recover.

As soon as he could ride horseback, he returned to Brazoria. He took his oath as minister before his neighbor, Chief Justice W.P. Scott. Then he set about arranging another year's absence from his home and office.

Jones left Texas in a depressed mood. He was leaving behind him all his earthly possessions — and Mary McCrory. The voyage did nothing to improve his mood. The three-day trip on the ship *Columbia* was rough and he was very seasick.

From New Orleans he boarded the steamer *Buckeye* for the trip up the Mississippi. For twenty-four days he was on uncomfortable riverboats, stagecoaches, and trains. In spite of the discomfort, his mood grew lighter as he traveled over new land. He kept a notebook handy to jot down his impressions of animals, plants, and people. While he was in Iowa he noted: "One fellow on board undertook to draw a comparison between Ioway *[sic]* and Texas — the man is a fool, for there is no comparison between them."

He arrived in Washington on August 23, 1838, ready to work for the Republic of Texas. He could not act in an official way until President Van Buren of the United States formally accepted him as minister of the Republic of Texas. Van Buren was unavailable until October 2, when he invited Minister Jones to the White House for a formal meeting.

Jones had not wasted time while he waited to be recognized. He contacted old acquaintances. He also called on the Bank of the United States in Philadelphia to open discussion about a five million dollar loan to Texas.

After he was "fully accredited" by President Van Buren, Jones began acting "officially." He "called with Cards" upon as many members of the Cabinet and Diplomatic Corps as he could in one afternoon.

He left a card engraved with his title, "Minister of the Republic of Texas," and name and address at the residence of each. A corner of each card was turned down to show it was delivered by Jones himself. He wanted the officials to know he knew Washington protocol and took his job seriously.

There were several jobs that President Houston wanted Jones to accomplish. One of the first tasks was to get a boundary agreement from the United States. Texas needed a clearly defined and marked boundary to be accepted by the United States and Europe as an independent country.

The second task was to assure the United States that Texas had withdrawn its request for annexation. The first proposal for annexation had been presented to the United States and voted down in 1837. Rumors were still flying about that Texas was trying to push annexation in spite of opposition.

Minister Jones wrote Chief Clerk A. Vail of the State Department on October 12, 1838:

Sir: . . . on the subject of the proposition to annex Texas to the United States, although that proposition was considered by this Government as finally disposed of, Texas has, never-the less, continued to be generally regarded by both countries as in the attitude of an applicant for admission into this Union . . . .

The undersigned, minister plenipotentiary of the republic of Texas, therefore, in accordance with his in-structions, has the honor to announce to the Secretary of State of the United States the formal and absolute with-drawal of the proposition of the annexation of Texas to the United States. . . .

Two major tasks were done. The next thing was to let Europe know about the decisions. Recognition of the Republic was not easy to obtain. In his last act as president of the United States, against great opposition, Andrew Jackson had recognized the Republic of Texas on March 3, 1837. That left Europe, which had to be convinced the Republic stood alone, free forever from Mexico. Europe held the key to the immediate future of Texas.

Jones created no great excitement in Washington. He was invited to state dinners, which were dull formal affairs. He dined with the president and Cabinet members when he was invited. He met with representatives of foreign countries as they heard the news that the Republic of Texas no longer desired annexation. Several dignitaries who had received his calling card began to return his visits.

Jones impressed them with the economic possibilities of Texas. The Republic had nearly two hundred million acres of land equal to any in the world. There were at least one hundred million acres of cotton land capable of producing enough to supply the world's demands. There were at least fifty million acres of natural pasture lands to raise better and cheaper beef and wool than any part of the United States. He predicted that Texas would add sugar to its productions and export vast amounts within a few years.

As if those things were not convincing enough, Jones added: "To say nothing, therefore, of the other natural resources of Texas, her mines, her mild and salubrious climate, etc., it cannot, I think, be denied by anyone, that she will shortly become an object of interest to European nations . . . and *may become*, to their great *commercial* and *manufacturing* interests."

While Jones waited in Washington for news from Europe, he knew only what he read in the newspapers about Texas. He was notified that Mirabeau Buonaparte Lamar had been inaugurated as the second president of the Republic of Texas. Jones assumed he would be called home immediately because he and Lamar had disagreed on too many issues. They did agree that annexation was a dead issue. Jones did not share Lamar's feelings that "annexation would be a disaster." He believed that annexation would be impossible unless American feelings against Texas changed. Jones would try to set forces in motion that might change those feelings.

President Lamar, who took office December 10, 1838, was a completely different administrator than ex-president Sam Houston. He immediately replaced most officials of government. Lamar wanted a new order in foreign and domestic affairs of the Republic. He set about to lay foundations for a nation that could remain forever independent. He filled political offices with people who supported his vision for the Republic. His first goal was to get an acknowledgment of Texas' independence from Mexico.

Jones had observed Lamar at different times for the past four years. He knew Lamar as an immigrant applying for land at Brazoria. They were both privates in the army until Lamar became a colonel when the Battle of San Jacinto began. And Lamar had presided over the Texas Senate when Jones was a congressman.

Jones, still in Washington, did not know if he was to continue work or return home. As he waited for communication from Texas, Jones wrote of Lamar: "He is a very weak man and governed by petty passions which he cannot control and by prejudices which are the result of ignorance."

His letter of dismissal arrived May 5, 1839. Jones was a private citizen again, and he was ready to go home.

He methodically inventoried his diplomatic wardrobe of nine coats, fourteen pantaloons, seven vests, one dozen shirts, three dozen collars, five black stocks, three pairs of boots, one of bootees, one of pumps, one of slippers, one morning wrapper, two hats, and "Stocking, Gloves, Hdkffs &c. &c innumerable." He spent two weeks visiting museums, theaters, and old friends while he waited for the *Viper* to take him to Texas.

Jones left Washington resolved to hold no public office "untill [sic] a change, and a radical one, is produced" in the Texan administration. When he arrived at the Galveston wharf, he learned that the Brazorians had elected him senator. His reception at Galveston was an expression of approval of his services abroad and the beginning of a political revolt against President Lamar.

He left for Houston to call upon the officials to terminate his ambassadorial career. His formal calls on the secretary of state and other officials of the Lamar administration made him once more a private citizen.

Jones had left Mary McCrory in Houston with promises to return. But he did not find her there. The Woodruff family had moved to Austin.

John Woodruff had moved his wife and children to Austin in June. The family camped for months, liv-

ing off buffalo meat. There were only two cabins under construction. Indians were a threat to the settlers
and had recently murdered thirteen men. The settlers
were building on the Indians' hunting grounds.

The Third Congress had decided to move the
capital of the Republic to Austin. Senator Jones was
against moving the government from Houston, but
the new Congress was to assemble there.

Texas could not afford to build a capitol befitting
its future greatness. A sprawling house for the use of
Congress and a smaller one for the president's office
were built. A two-story executive mansion was built
on a hill east of Congress Avenue. Sturdy little cabins for the government departments faced each
other along "the Avenue." In wet weather, clerks
traveled between offices on horseback. During October, forty ox wagons unloaded their cargoes of pa-
pers and furniture so the Texas government could
function again.

Anson Jones reached Austin on the last day of
October to find "no room nor bed to be had for love or
money." Edwin Waller, a fellow Brazorian, finally
rented him a room at his house. Jones immediately
set about acquiring land. Before winter was over, he
had bought over twenty choice lots for about $8,000.

On November 1, Jones finally saw Mary Mc-
Crory. The meeting was a disappointment for both of
them. It had been over a year since they had met.
Both of them had changed. Neither was eager to begin their engagement again.

Senator Jones turned his energies toward politics. He was the only Texas senator with any experience in diplomacy. The chairmanship of the committee on foreign relations fell to him. In his first

report on foreign relations, he urged his colleagues to support President Lamar. Lamar was trying to negotiate peace with Mexico.

Mexico still had not recognized Texas independence. The plan was to offer Mexico five million dollars for a clear title to the land between the Nueces and Rio Grande. Jones pointed out that war with Mexico would cost more than five million dollars. Loss of human lives and the chaos of another war on Texas soil could not be measured, he reasoned. On the other hand, if peace were assured by Mexico, land values would increase "at least fourfold" within five years. Joint resolutions passed on Jones' recommendation.

The Senate adjourned on February 5, 1840, and Jones turned again to his personal life. He had bought several plots of land in and around Austin. He became Anson Jones, M.D., and placed a sign on his door. He began courting Mary McCrory in earnest.

There were constant alarms of Indian and Mexican invasion, but Jones pushed ahead to build a cottage on Pecan Street. He found Mary to be a pleasant and comfortable companion. They resumed their plans of 1838 when he had been called to Washington. Mary had been collecting her wedding trousseau for over two years. It was now complete. Also, Jones' house on Pecan Street was finished, and his public duties were temporarily over. There was no reason to delay marriage.

Dr. Jones bought the second marriage license issued in Travis County. He paid Chief Justice Smith $50 to perform the ceremony.

Dr. Anson Jones of Brazoria married Mary McCrory on May 17, 1840. He was content with his life.

Chapter 12

Secretary of State Jones

*"I [Sam Houston] will assure you that you
will find worthy associates in the cabinet....
Don't say you are 'poor.' I am — all are so!"*

S enator and Mrs. Jones became a part of the
social life of Austin. His professional life was
prosperous. He was accumulating wealth in money
and in land. Mary was expecting their first child.
Life was good for him.

He took his seat in the Fifth Congress "rather
mechanically." There were many personal feuds
among the congressmen. Jones felt that the problems concerning the Republic were more important
than getting into petty quarrels.

President Lamar had dreams and plans for the
Republic. But Texas was in debt. There was no
money for education, transportation, or trade. President Lamar had created many problems to be solved.
People, including Sam Houston, were upset over his
policies. By the end of Lamar's term and the ad-
journing of the Fifth Congress, Jones wondered if
the shaky Republic would survive.

Once again, Jones decided to leave politics behind and begin a private life with his family. He sold his house on Pecan Street and bought a $900 carriage to take him and Mary from Austin. Mary was due to deliver their first child any day, and Jones was nervous. He had delivered many children during his years as a physician. For the first time he understood why new fathers behaved as they did.

On February 26, 1841, "about a quarter past one in the morning [his] Son Saml Houston was born. . . ." Jones passed out "about twenty dollars worth of Cigars." A month later he put Mary and Sam Houston in the new carriage and headed toward Brazoria. He said that anyone was welcome to his seat in Congress. He wanted to be plain Anson Jones, M.D. He planned a future without politics. But politics was in his blood.

The political campaign for President Lamar's replacement was a bitter fight between Sam Houston and David G. Burnet. Houston poked fun at Burnet. Burnet said Houston was a drunkard. Many thought the campaign was a disgrace. Others shook their heads and said, "Politics as usual!"

Dr. Jones was ready to leave all that behind. Brazoria was as good a place as any to watch the developments. It was also a good place to avoid political discussions.

The Jones family reached Brazoria County on April 11. Mary and little Sam stayed in Columbia while Dr. Jones visited former patients and old political friends. He spent two weeks visiting along the Brazos and San Bernard rivers and on to Houston and Galveston. He needed medical supplies, but political leaders needed him.

Dr. Jones returned to Columbia at the end of April "willing to make the race for vice-president." A week later, at a political rally at the courthouse in Columbia, John W. Cloud said, "The Hon. Anson Jones is prominently deserving of his country's suffrages, from his own intrinsic talents, from his correct affections; and from being Gen Houston's choice!"

While Jones waited for developments in his race for vice-president, he opened an office in Columbia. Between visits with patients he read "a hundred or more" letters from men all over Texas asking him to tour the Republic and campaign for office.

At the capital, President Lamar was taking a last great gamble. He would end his presidency with a successful expedition to Santa Fe. Santa Fe was in New Mexico territory, which Mexico still claimed. There were rumors that Santa Fe would like to join Texas. President Lamar wanted to control Santa Fe to show the Mexican government that Texans meant business. Texans also wanted to control Santa Fe trade.

When Lamar had requested funds to finance the expedition, he was turned down by the Fifth Congress. Now Congress had adjourned, and he had no one to stop him. He believed that a successful march on Santa Fe would solve most of Texas' economic problems. He never thought of failure.

President Lamar organized the expedition himself. Merchants took goods to trade. Officials went along to help organize a Texas government in Santa Fe. Some adventurous Texans went along for the excitement. But they did not get the welcome Lamar had wanted. The New Mexicans did not want to be under the rule of Texas or Mexico.

Members of the expedition were arrested and taken to Mexico. They were thrown into prison in Perote, where they remained almost a year. The Mexican government was convinced that Texas wanted more land, not just peace.

The Santa Fe expedition increased difficulties between Texas and Mexico. Lamar's great scheme had failed. He had created more problems for Texas. Mexico was very suspicious and angry.

A. C. Hyde wrote Jones from the capital: "Everything here is alive with the Santa Fe expedition, which will . . . cost the Government about half a million. Things are getting on worse than ever in the departments, they are paying no attention to any of the acts of Congress. It is an awful state of things that our Government should be in the hands of such men . . . ."

Jones agreed with Hyde. He decided that his original decision to retire from politics was the right one. He went to Houston to explain to his friends: "The sacrifice is too great. I do not wish the office; I have not the means to spare; and if I had, I am opposed 'toto coelo' to such a course [electioneering]. Propriety, therefore, requires me to decline."

He returned to his office in Columbia. He settled his family and servant at Mr. Ammon Underwood's and devoted himself to his family and patients. It was good to be a country doctor — and profitable too.

Jones was not surprised when Sam Houston won his second term as president of the Texas Republic. Houston had laid out his plans for Texas. He planned to cut the cost of government. He wanted to stop the trouble with the Native Texans (Indians). He planned to work to have Texas join the United States.

As soon as his victory was announced, Houston decided who he wanted in his Cabinet. He wrote to Anson Jones: "Now all this preface is to ask you if you will be so good as to accept the station of Secretary of State. . . . I assure you that you will find worthy associates in the cabinet."

Jones had gone to Austin to clear some titles at the General Land Office. Houston's letter went to Brazoria and back to Austin. It arrived a week before Houston was inaugurated. The office of secretary of state was tempting. But, Jones reasoned to himself, he had to support a family, and his practice was making good money.

After a week of meetings with President-elect Houston and others selected for positions in the new Cabinet, Jones wrote of his decision: "I was solicited, urged; implored, and finally persuaded. . . ." On inauguration day, December 1, 1841, Jones wrote his wife that he had "consented to accept the Office of Secretary of State, temporarily."

Houston constructed the Cabinet around Jones. He had seen Jones change from a small country doctor to a confident man of affairs. He had watched Jones at San Jacinto, in Congress, as minister to the United States, and in the Texas Senate. Houston could use Jones' firsthand knowledge of diplomacy and his analytical, cautious mind.

Secretary Jones became a permanent roomer in Austin with Major Asa Brigham. Mary and Sam Houston Jones (whom his father called "the young Secretary of State") stayed in Brazoria. Jones thought his office in government was temporary. Austin was still a rugged, undeveloped town. Living conditions were primitive for those who had not built a home. The Indians were a constant threat. There was also talk that the capital would be moved again.

Jones decided not to move his family back to Austin. He wrote Mary in February 1942: "It affords me a good excuse for taking *leave of absence* for awhile, & I want to get away from here so bad that I am scarcely in a good humor any part of the time."

Among Secretary Jones' worries was what to do about the failed Santa Fe expedition. Rumors reached Austin that Texans had been imprisoned in Mexico. Texans were angry and wanted to claim the land by force. Jones was caught in the middle. He still believed that Texas had two choices: to be recognized by Mexico, Paris, and London as an independent Republic, or to annex to the United States. Texas had to make some choices before it became bankrupt or entered into war with Mexico.

Little was accomplished during the first session of the Sixth Congress. Jones was glad it adjourned on February 9, 1842. He had not seen his family since October. President Houston gave Jones a leave of absence to encourage him to continue as secretary of state. Mary and the "young secretary of state" were waiting for him at "Cousin Oliver's plantation on the Brazos."

All along the road to his family he heard rumors that Mexico was sending an army into Texas. Before he could take Mary and baby Sam back to Brazoria, he received a message from President Houston. The president was calling together all of his advisers in

Houston. Santa Anna, again president of Mexico, was sending troops back to Texas. He planned to show the Republic that it still belonged to Mexico.

When Houston succeeded Lamar, every program was cut to save money. Congress had enacted a "retrenchment plan" which disbanded the Texas army. Now all they had was a group of untrained and angry volunteers. The government had no control or direction of them. Jones saw diplomacy as the only way out. Texas was ill-prepared to fight Mexico again.

Mexico had not recognized Texas' independence, but the great powers of the world had: the United States in 1837, France in 1839, and England in 1840. Secretary Jones sent Ashbel Smith to Europe to assist the English, French, Belgian, and German impresarios (colonizing agents) "to bring population and Money to Texas from the storehouses of Europe." Colonies of Europeans between the Rio Grande and Texas settlements would serve as a buffer against Mexican attacks. It would take time and patience, but Jones believed this was the way to independence.

Mexico did not have patience. Santa Anna sent troops to Texas. They took San Antonio, Goliad, and Refugio by surprise. They held the towns for several days. The Texans thought it was a major invasion. Settlers on the frontier fled to the East for safety.

Houston called Congress into a special session. By the time they all gathered, the Mexicans were gone. An angry Congress declared war. Houston knew that Texas was unprepared and would likely lose to Mexico. He vetoed the declaration of war.

In September 1842 the Mexican army again invaded Texas by surprise. They took over San Antonio for more than a week and then left abruptly. The Texans were angry. They thought Houston was wrong. About 300 Texans gathered to invade Mexico. They would not listen to orders. They marched to Mier and captured the town. But the Mexican army attacked and took the Texans as prisoners.

The Texans were marched to Mexico and placed in prison. Santa Anna ruled that one out of every ten Texans would be shot. The prisoners had to choose which ones were to die. The soldiers placed white and black beans in a pot. There were seventeen black ones. The men who drew black beans were shot. The rest remained in prison until September 1844.

The chaos and confusion among Texans was reflected in the government. President Houston wanted to move the capital back to Houston. Jones and others thought it should remain in a central location. Houston called Congress to convene in Houston and ordered government records to be moved. But citizens in Austin stood guard at the capitol and refused to allow the archives to leave.

Jones disagreed with some of President Houston's political policies. He was despondent over how slowly things were moving. He was also tired and ill. Houston gave him a leave of absence to rest and recover. When he did start to Houston, he learned that the president "had packed up and gone to Washington-on - the-Brazos."

Jones returned to Columbia, where he had "left Mrs. Jones and Sam at Dr. Phelps's." He would remain there "until the government took a notion to light." He needed time to organize his thoughts about the future of the Republic. And he needed to plan his own future in or out of politics.

Chapter 13

Last President of the Republic

"I have a vitally important object to accomplish in completing the salvation and safety of the country. . . ."

P resident Sam Houston declared Washington-on-the-Brazos, Texas, "the constitutional capital." Washington had one hotel which was soon overflowing. Everyone with more than one room took in lodgers. The president's office was a one room log law office with a fireplace, one couch, one table, and one chair.

Secretary of State Anson Jones was across the street in a clapboard building that had once been a carpenter's shop. He left Mary and little Sam at Dr. Phelps' plantation until he could decide what he wanted to do in the future. He could quit politics completely and live a very relaxed and comfortable life with his family and medical practice. Or he could move Mary and Sam to a new plantation house near Washington and plan to run for the presidency of the Republic of Texas in 1844.

People began to tell Secretary Jones that they

were sick of the silly quarrels at the capitol. Some said he would make a better president than Sam Houston. The election was nearly two years away. But Texans started choosing their next candidate as soon as the current president was inaugurated. Even some of Houston's friends said Jones could carry out Houston's objectives better than the "Old Chief" himself.

In December 1842 the Seventh Congress convened after several days of not having enough members for a quorum. Jones was becoming dissatisfied with Houston's leadership. Houston criticized Congress. Congress criticized Houston. Nothing was accomplished. Jones felt it was Houston's fault. Houston seemed to deliberately disagree on everything. It was as if he set out to make people dislike him. Jones felt Houston was going too far.

Everything Houston wanted was rejected by the House of Representatives. They refused to buy furniture for the president's house in Washington. They declined to order the archives brought from Austin to Washington. They would not change the time and place of meeting of the Supreme Court. In general, they refused all of his requests and recommendations.

During the congressional season, Anson Jones was facing personal problems and decisions. His salary had dropped drastically in the past two years while his expenses had grown. Mary was expecting their second child. His board bill was more than he made as secretary of state. He needed money. Instead of making an immediate decision, Jones tried to be all things. He took his medical bag and made the rounds of the plantations as often as he could. He continued as secretary of state the rest of the time.

In January 1843 Jones decided to move his family to Washington. He was tired of "camping." He wanted Mary and the "young secretary of state" with him. He took them to Mr. Farquhar's plantation three miles from Washington.

The prosperous plantation had several advantages for Jones. He was too far from Washington for everyone to bother him. And he had time to think and work. When he was needed in town, one of his slaves, who was porter of the Department of State, rode out for him. Jones enjoyed learning about the new plantation. He had dreams of having one of his own one day. He enjoyed spending time with Mary and little Sam.

When Jones had to spend time in Washington, Mary sometimes went with him and stayed with Margaret Houston. Although Mary had disapproved of naming their son after Sam Houston, the two young women had many things in common. Both had young children and were pregnant again. Both had husbands in government service. Both spent a good deal of time separated from their husbands. They had the courage and stamina of frontier women. Neither became involved in politics.

Secretary Jones remained quiet on issues that he thought were "petty warfare." He felt that the Texans had "begged [the United States] long enough" for annexation. There were other options they could choose. His plan was to open alternatives.

Within Texas, two major issues had to be settled. There was a large group of anti-Houston politicians. There were also hostile Indians, and Houston knew how to deal with the Indians. He sent agents to all the chiefs inviting them to Washington-on-the-Brazos for a powwow. As the chiefs arrived, they set up camp in a shady grove on the road to Jones' house. Indian agents took the camp beef and corn. The men lay on buffalo robes, smoking pipes that looked like tomahawks, while their wives did the work.

When the chiefs began to get restless, Houston took his Cabinet and led them in formation to the camp. The staff had been instructed not to speak. The president would do all of the talking and they were to follow his lead.

The chiefs and officials sat in a huge circle around a long-stemmed, ceremonial stone pipe that Houston had had carved for the occasion. President Houston signaled for the pipe to be filled with tobacco and lighted. With dramatic movements Houston took the pipe, pulled a puff of smoke into his mouth, lifted his eyes to the sky, and slowly exhaled. Then the pipe was passed to the oldest chief. Each man in the circle took a puff with "prayers to that Power which upholds nations and rules their destinies, that our troubles might come to an end."

Secretary Jones was impressed with Houston. He agreed with Houston that peace with the Native Americans was more humane and cheaper than warfare. The chiefs promised to be peaceful and left with their gifts. Jones and Houston turned their energies to dealing once again with the white men.

Texas was in economic trouble. Houston had reduced government expenses. Salaries were reduced,

and many offices were closed. The army did not receive pay. The ships of the Texas Navy were put up for sale.

There was more and more talk about annexation. Slavery had been a main problem between Texas and the United States. Andrew Jackson, Sam Houston's friend, had faced the problem in 1836. The slavery issue had delayed recognition of Texas' independence. Texas was a slave state, and many Americans did not want another slave state in the Union. They fought against annexation. John Tyler, a Southerner, became president of the United States in 1841. He supported the annexation of Texas. A proposal was presented to Congress and voted down.

Sam Houston lost popularity among the Texans. By Texas law, he could not succeed himself as president. Houston's friends and opponents thought Secretary Jones was the one to follow Houston. Neither Jones nor Houston commented on their opinions. Jones wanted to be sure he was supported by the right people before he committed himself.

Moses Johnson, M.D., of Independence, wrote Jones in July 1843: "I think he [President Houston] would be glad to see you succeed him, for he thinks you the greatest man in Texas, or nearly so." Jones wasn't sure if Houston's approval would help or hurt him politically. He was not ready to declare himself as a candidate. He also believed there were others who would be stronger candidates. He decided not to seek the office but not to decline it if he were offered it.

At this point in his life, Jones had personal interests that needed attention. Mary was expecting their second child and was very nervous. Jones spent most of his time at the Farquhar plantation. He helped take care of Mary and played with little Sam. On September 4, 1843, a second son was born. Jones had named Sam after President Sam Houston against Mary's wishes. This time he offered to let her name the new son, thinking she would name him Anson after himself. Much to his surprise — and disappointment — she named the new arrival Charles Elliot, after a British diplomat.

Jones continued to receive letters asking whether he was going to campaign for the presidency. He was reluctant to make a decision. He knew that the Texan legislators "were afflicted with annexation fever." Jones kept silent on his views but felt "the most we can hope for is *Independence*."

He rented Cooke's plantation next to his own land, which he had named "Barrington" after the town in which he was born. He "contracted with Mr. John Campbell to build a house, kitchen, and smokehouse" on his land and began farming.

While he was busy with his plantation, personal relations between him and Houston became strained. Jones felt Houston was taking over his diplomatic job. Houston was beginning to wonder if Jones was the man to follow him.

Texas became a political issue in the United States. The United States feared that the British would support and take over Texas. Mexico had not officially given up Texas. President Tyler signed a quick treaty with Texas and presented it to the U.S. Senate. The Senate rejected the treaty. Texas stood alone without total independence.

Anson Jones was discouraged. He became a passive candidate for president of the Republic. When he was criticized for his lack of enthusiasm, he wrote: "I do not mean to be understood that I am indifferent *to the honor* of being elected to the office of the Pres . . . . I had not sought the nomination. . . . it is now my humble opinion too late in the day for a change."

Jones became angry when he was accused of running for president on "another man's popularity," meaning Houston's. He replied to one critic, "I *have never been beaten* in my life for any office, — nor do I ever intend to be. . . ." When his supporters understood that Jones was in the race to win, they began campaigning for him. Many believed that the future of Texas lay in the continuation of Jones' policies of working for independence and annexation at the same time. Many of his opponents accused him of being against annexation. Some said he wanted England to rule Texas.

To get away from the stress of campaigning, Jones returned to his plantation. He spent the days before the election working his land and overseeing the building of his house on Barrington.

On September 4, 1844, Texans went to the polls again to elect a president. On that day Anson Jones went from country doctor, revolutionary soldier, legislator, diplomat, senator, and cabinet officer to president. He had come a long way from the immigrant in 1833 to the "First Citizen" of the nation he had helped to create.

President Jones was a man of influence. He had financial security and land in several counties. He was building a plantation home that would soon become the "White House of the Republic." He had a loving wife, two bright and healthy sons, and another child was expected.

Jones and Texas had grown together. A hundred thousand people had come to Texas since his arrival. Cities and towns had sprung up in open country. Schools and churches were being built. Brick and clapboard houses replaced log cabins. Houses were furnished with imported goods from the United States and Europe. Along the frontier, settlers from the United States, England, France, and Germany were establishing homesteads. And more were coming.

Between the time of the election and President-elect Jones' inauguration on December 9, 1844, the government was basically inactive. Annexation was at a standstill. Everyone watched the United States presidential election. The two candidates were James A. Polk and Henry Clay. Polk wanted to annex Texas. Clay did not. When Polk won, annexation seemed certain.

From the first mention of annexation, Jones had aimed at getting a choice for Texans: annexation or independence. He had pursued both at the same time. As president he was not going to be pressured into changing his policies. He did not address the problem immediately.

He turned instead to the general problems of an independent nation. Time had come to abandon paper money, to reduce expenses, and to tax lightly but collect all taxes assessed. The president thought the people should decide by vote where the seat of government should be for the next twenty years. He asked for no money for an army or navy. Texas rangers would protect the frontier. The land system needed to be simplified, a penal code written, and a lighthouse built at Galveston. President Jones' program aimed solely at problems that had to be solved regardless of annexation or independence.

As the Eighth Congress tried to deal with government problems, President Jones had a greater concern. Mary was expecting their third child and seemed more nervous than before. All of the duties of getting the Barrington place ready fell to her. She was a robust and sensible woman, but the worries of the presidential campaign, the house building on Barrington, and her pregnancy had increased her anxiety. She wanted her husband with her.

President Jones was relieved and overjoyed when his daughter Sarah was born before midnight on January 8, 1845. He stayed on the plantation several days after her birth. When he was sure Mary and Sarah were doing well, he returned to Washington. He took a room in town to remain during the rest of the congressional season.

When Congress adjourned in February in Texas, there was a full debate going on in Washington. Texas annexation was the topic of discussion. In his last days of office, President Tyler signed a resolution to annex Texas. The resolution was approved by the United States Senate.

While Texans waited to hear the final approval, President and Mrs. Jones moved from the plantation house to Barrington. They planted "fruit and ornamental Trees & other things" around their new house. President Jones found relief from the stresses of his office by farming and spending time with his growing family.

He did not want to rush into annexation without first acquiring Texas' independence. He could not discuss official dealings with England, France, and Mexico until there were definite treaty offers. Rumors spread throughout Texas. People did not understand his secrecy. Overnight he became a hated man. He was burned in effigy, but he still remained silent. People began to believe that he opposed annexation.

When Jones learned in early June that Mexico was ready to sign a treaty, he was ready to offer Texans "the alternatives of peace with the world and Independence, or annexation and its contingencies." He was ready to call for a vote. Congress reassembled on June 16. He presented to Congress the treaties of England, France, and Mexico and annexation to the United States. They voted unanimously to accept the offer of annexation. A special convention was called. The Convention of 1845 accepted the offer on July 4, 1845. It also wrote a new state constitution.

Texans voted on October 13, 1845, to accept annexation and to adopt the new constitution. President James A. Polk approved the vote. On December 29, 1845, Texas became a state of the United States.

On February 1, 1846, President Jones returned to Austin, the official capital of the state of Texas. Preparations were being made for the Republic of Texas' final act. A platform was built beside the door of Representative Hall. A mounted cannon stood guard on President Hill. Flags decorated the building. A new flagpole was placed by the old wooden one.

As President Jones looked out the window of his room, he was overcome with emotion. He tore up the speech he had prepared, "a rather so so affair," and started over. His speech captured so well what he felt that he did not need notes to make it.

At noon on February 19, 1846, President Jones, Governor-elect J. Pinckney Henderson, and joint committees of the two houses were escorted on stage by United States Army officers. After being introduced, President Jones rose, went to the lectern, and delivered his last speech:

> The great measure of annexation, so earnestly desired by the people of Texas, is happily consummated. The present occasion ... [is] the most extraordinary in the annals of the world, and one which marks a bright triumph in the history of republican institutions. . . .
>
> I, as President of the Republic with my officers, am now present to surrender into the hands of those whom the people have chosen, the power and the authority which we have some time held. This surrender is made with the most perfect cheerfulness. . . . I lay down the honors and the cares of the Presidency with infinitely more of person gratification than I assumed them.
>
> . . . May the Union be perpetual, and may it be the means of conferring benefits and blessings upon the people of all the States, is my ardent prayer.
>
> The final act in this great drama is now performed. The Republic of Texas is no more.

It was so quiet, people heard the president's footsteps as he stepped to the flagpole. He lowered the banner of his Republic. The rotted, wooden pole broke in two as the flag came down. The cannon on

President Hill boomed across the silence in a salute to the newest American state. The United States flag was slowly raised to the cheers of the crowd.

Anson Jones, the fourth and last president of the Republic of Texas, had delivered Texas to the United States.

The Republic of Texas *was* no more.

Afterword

". . . somehow or the other the destiny of Texas was interwoven with my own."

Anson Jones had finished his mission. He retired to Barrington, where he grew cotton, corn, and tobacco. He was a successful plantation owner as he had dreamed he would be. He watched his children grow.

Sam, whose name was changed to Samuel Edward when Jones fell out with Houston, was interested in scientific things. Charles was an excellent student. Sarah, or Sissy as her father called her, was like her mother — quiet, capable and responsible. Cromwell Anson, named after his most notable ancestor, was born in 1850. He was full of mischief and curiosity. Their Aunt Mary from New York lived with them and taught the children their lessons.

Jones and his wife entertained many important guests in the beautiful plantation home they had created. He decided to stay out of politics. The only way he would leave his plantation would be to go to

Washington as a senator from Texas. He spent time working on a manuscript about his life in politics when he was not overseeing his plantation.

One day in 1849 he was brought home unconscious, his left arm limp and purple. His horse had thrown him. Anson's arm never recovered from the fall. It remained useless and a constant source of pain. He could not find a cure for it in Texas, Philadelphia, or New York. From then until the end of his life, he never left the house without gloves to hide his withered and discolored hand. He found nothing to take away the pain.

In 1857 Jones was approached to run for the Senate. He told everyone who asked him about it that he "never sought office, but would accept if the people called" him. When he lost the election, he decided to move from Barrington to Galveston. Barrington was sold.

In Galveston he announced that he would practice medicine. He rented a house and returned to Houston, to stay at the Old Capitol Hotel, which had once been the capitol of Texas. The hotel reminded him that "somehow or the other the destiny of Texas was interwoven with my own."

To a friend who visited with Jones that night, he said, "My public career . . . began in this house; and I have been thinking it might close here." Jones was found dead the next morning, January 9, 1858.

He had left his completed manuscript with a banker in Galveston. Mary did not read it but sent it to a New York publisher. The first edition of *Memoranda and Official Correspondence Relating to the Republic of Texas* was published in 1859. Mrs. Jones never remarried and lived in Houston with her daughter Sarah until her death on December 31, 1907.

Barrington, "the White House of Washington-on-the-Brazos," was moved from its original location to Washington-on-the-Brazos State Historical Park in 1936. The historic home was restored and furnished by the Barrington Society in 1970. The park, site of the signing of the Texas Declaration of Independence on March 2, 1836, is located on the rolling banks of the Brazos River. Deeply rooted cypress and pecan trees, swaying in the wind on the banks of the river, remind visitors of the wild, independent spirits of those unforgotten Texans who gave us our heritage.

Anson Jones is one of those unforgotten Texans. The last president of the Republic will always be remembered as "the Architect of Annexation." The hope he expressed in his last speech as president has been fulfilled: ". . . the public mind will settle down into proper conclusions. . . . [and I] repose upon the assured belief that history and prosperity will do me no wrong."

Timeline of Anson Jones

January 20, 1798 — Anson Jones born at Seekonkville, Great Barrington, Massachusetts.

September 5, 1820 — Jones received title of doctor.

October 1820 — Jones set up practice in Bainbridge, Connecticut.

January 1821 — Moses Austin's land grant approved to colonize Texas.

1821 — Jones moved to Norwich, Connecticut, to open a drugstore. Moses Austin died and Stephen F. Austin took his place.

1822 — Jones arrested in Philadelphia for bad debts.

1824 — Jones moved to Venezuela to practice medicine. By the end of year, 300 families were established in Texas.

1825 — Stephen F. Austin applied for second land grant to establish 300 more families in Texas. The government approved 500 families.

1826 — Jones returned to Philadelphia to practice medicine and study at Jefferson Medical College.

1827 — Jones graduated from medical college and joined a Masonic Lodge.

April 6, 1830 — Mexico passed a law to stop the westward movement of people from the United States to Texas.

1832 — Mexico passed new colonization law that angered Texans.

October 1832 — Jones sailed on the ship *Alabama* to New Orleans to become a businessman. The Texans held a convention to elect their own state government.

April 1, 1833 — Texans held second convention and adopted a state constitution. Austin took it to Mexico and was imprisoned.

October 1833 — Jones sailed on the ship *Sabine* for Texas.

November 1, 1833 — Jones arrived in Brazoria and set up medical practice.

1834 — Jones became a successful doctor and began to accumulate wealth.

1835 — Mexico reestablished custom houses. Mexican General Cós came to Texas to restore order.

Summer 1835 — Jones signed petitions for the convening of a delegation to declare independence.

September 1835 — Jones met Stephen F. Austin, who declared, "War is our only resource." Austin had been released from a Mexico prison after two years there.

October 2, 1835 — First battle of the Revolution at Gonzales over a cannon.

November 3, 1835 — Convention held at San Felipe which organized a provisional government.

December 1835 — Jones wrote resolutions in favor of a "Declaration of Independence from Mexico" which was published Christmas Day.

January 1836 — Colonel James C. Neil commanded the Alamo. Santa Anna began march to Texas.

February 1836 — Jim Bowie, who commanded the volunteers, and William Barret Travis, who commanded the regulars, refused to destroy the Alamo.

February 1, 1836 — Jones "declined all requests to become a candidate" as a delegate to the "Convention of the People of Texas at Washington-on-the-Brazos."

February 23, 1836 — Santa Anna began a thirteen-day siege on the Alamo. Travis wrote famous "Victory or Death" letter.

March 1, 1836 — Convention of the People of Texas at Washington-on-the-Brazos drafted a statement of independence.

March 2, 1836 — Texas was declared an independent republic.

March 6, 1836 — Battle of the Alamo.

March 16, 1836 — Jones put in a claim for a league and a labor (4,605 acres) of land.

March 19, 1836 — Jones left Brazoria to join Houston's army. Fannin and his command surrendered to General Urea's army at Battle of Coleta.

March 24, 1836 — Jones joined Houston's army as a private.

March 27, 1836 — Colonel James Walker Fannin and his command (about 390 Americans) were massacred near Goliad.

102

April 1836 — Jones was appointed "surgeon to the 2d Regiment." Houston continued to retreat eastward.

April 19, 1836 — Houston marched toward enemy at San Jacinto. Jones disobeyed orders and went with troops.

April 21, 1836 — Battle of San Jacinto. Houston was shot in the leg.

May 5, 1836 — Jones was appointed apothecary general.

September 1836 — Sam Houston was elected president of the Republic.

June 1837 — Jones petitioned Congress for a Medical Society Board of Medical Censors. The bill died before Congress adjourned.

September 4, 1837 — Jones was elected to the Second Congress.

September 25, 1837 — Second Congress convened in Houston. Jones was chairman of several committees. Medical bill to regulate the medical profession in Texas was passed.

May 1838 — Anson Jones became engaged to Mary Smith McCrory.

June 1838 — Jones was appointed minister plenipotentiary to the United States and postponed marriage.

August 23, 1838 — Jones arrived in Washington.

December 10, 1838 — Mirabeau Buonaparte Lamar became second president of the Republic of Texas.

May 5, 1839 — Jones was relieved of Washington duties to become a private citizen again.

June 1839 — Capitol of Republic was moved from Houston to Austin.

September 1839 — Jones was elected senator from Brazoria.

October 1839 — Jones moved to Austin, where he bought property and began building a house on Pecan Street.

February 5, 1840 — Senate adjourned and Jones returned to private practice.

May 17, 1840 — Jones married Mary Smith McCrory.

February 26, 1841 — Samuel Houston, first son of Joneses, was born.

April 1841 — Jones joined the race for vice-president of the Republic.

June 1841 — Lamar's Santa Fe expedition.

August 1841 — Jones withdrew from vice-presidential race.

September 1841 — Sam Houston was elected third president of the Republic of Texas.

December 1, 1841 — Jones was appointed secretary of state.

December 1842 — President Houston moved the capital to Washington-on-the-Brazos.

January 1843 — Jones moved his family to Washington.

September 4, 1843 — Second son, Charles Elliot, was born to Joneses.

September 2, 1844 — Anson Jones was elected the fourth and last president of the Republic of Texas.

January 8, 1845 — Joneses' daughter Sarah was born.

February 1845 — The Jones family moved to Barrington — The White House of Texas.

June 1845 — Mexico signed treaty with Texas recognizing the republic's independence.

June 16, 1845 — Congress voted to accept offer of annexation.

October 13, 1845 — Texans voted to annex to the United States and to accept a new constitution.

December 29, 1845 — Texas became the twenty-eighth state in the United States.

February 19, 1846 — Ceremony lowering the Republic flag and raising the United States flag.

February 1846 — Jones returned to Barrington to oversee his plantation and to write his *Memoranda and Official Correspondence Relating to the Republic of Texas and Annexation, Including a Brief Autobiography of the Author.*

1849 — Jones suffered irreparable injury to his left arm when his horse fell on him.

1850 — Joneses' third son Cromwell Anson was born.

1857 — Jones sold Barrington.

January 9, 1858 — Jones died in the Old Capitol Hotel in Houston.

1859 — His *Memoranda . . .* was published.

December 31, 1907 — Mary Smith McCrory Jones died in Houston.

Bibliography

Anson Jones Collection. Archives and Manuscripts Collection. Center for American History. University of Texas at Austin.

Carroll, H. Bailey, and others. *Heroes of Texas.* Waco, Texas: Texian Press, 1966.

Connor, Seymour V., and others. *Capitols of Texas.* Waco, Texas: Texian Press, 1970.

Crawford, Ann Fears, and others. *Texas — Lone Star Land: Its History, Its Geography, Its Government, Its People.* Austin: W.S. Benson & Company, Inc., 1993.

Dixon, Sam Houston, and Louis Wiltz Kemp. *The Heroes of San Jacinto.* Houston, Texas: The Anson Jones Press, 1932.

Fehrenbach, T.R. *Lone Star: A History of Texas and the Texans.* New York: The Macmillan Company, 1969.

———. *Seven Keys to Texas.* University of Texas at El Paso: Texas Western Press, 1983.

Flynn, Jean. *Stephen F. Austin: Father of Texas.* Austin: Eakin Press, 1981.

Gambrell, Herbert. *Anson Jones: The Last President of Texas.* Austin: University of Texas Press, 1964.

Jones, Anson. *Memoranda and Official Correspondence Relating to the Republic of Texas and Annexation, Including a Brief Autobiography of the Author.* New York: D. Appleton and Company, 1859.

Kerr, Rita. *Texas Footprints: Austin's Old Three Hundred.* Austin: Eakin Press, 1990.

Rather, Ethel Zivley. "Recognition of the Republic of Texas by the United States." *The Quarterly of the Texas State Historical Association,* Vol. 13, January 1910.

Reichstein, Andreas V., with trans. by Jeanne R. Willson. *Rise of the Lone Star: The Making of Texas.* College Station: Texas A & M University Press, 1989.

Webb, Walter Prescott, and H. Bailey Carroll (eds.). *The Handbook of Texas.* 2 vols. Austin: Texas State Historical Association, 1952.